The Excesses of God

Robinson Jeffers as a Religious Figure

✦

Is it not by his high superfluousness we know
Our God? For to equal a need
Is natural, animal, mineral: but to fling
Rainbows over the rain,
And beauty above the moon, and secret rainbows
On the domes of deep sea-shells,
And make the necessary embrace of breeding
Beautiful also as fire,
Not even the weeds to multiply without blossom
Nor the birds without music:
There is the great humaneness at the heart of things,
The extravagant kindness, the fountain
Humanity can understand, and would flow likewise
If power and desire were perch-mates.

                              The Excesses of God

WILLIAM EVERSON

✦

THE
EXCESSES
OF
GOD

Robinson Jeffers as a
Religious Figure

✦

WITH A FOREWORD BY
ALBERT GELPI

1988
STANFORD UNIVERSITY PRESS
STANFORD, CALIFORNIA

Stanford University Press, Stanford, California
© 1988 by the Board of Trustees of the
Leland Stanford Junior University

Printed in the United States of America
CIP data appear at the end of the book

To
Robert Hawley,
Man of Books

Contents

Foreword, by Albert Gelpi   ix

Preface   xiii

Introduction   1

ONE   All Flesh Is Grass   9

TWO   The Wine Cup of This Fury   47

THREE   And After the Fire a Still Small Voice   93

FOUR   The Horseleech Hath Two Daughters   127

Conclusion   167

"The Poet Is Dead"   171

Notes   181

Index   187

✦

Foreword

Robert Zaller called his recent critical study of Robinson Jeffers—
with metaphorical aptness—*The Cliffs of Solitude*. Jeffers with-
drew from urban centers and literary vortices in flinty and reso-
lute alienation from the prevailing values in commercial society
and in Modernist art. He found his poetic voice by rooting him-
self in his marriage to Una Call Kuster and rooting that marriage
in the stretch of California coast from Monterey to Big Sur: hence
the erotically charged pantheism which this book seeks to eluci-
date. The stone house and tower he built by hand with his twin
sons on a promontory above the sea outside (at the time) the town
of Carmel symbolized his rugged, individualistic isolation.

Jeffers's poetic stance was programmatically opposed to the
Modernism of Eliot and Stevens, Pound and Williams, and be-
spoke a Romanticism darkened by his Calvinist temperament,
Darwinian science, and Lucretian materialism. His nature mys-
ticism found its ethical and social expression in the philosophical
position he called Inhumanism. He did not know or correspond
with the poets or critics who set the norms and filled the pages
of the literary journals. He did not give many readings or teach
on college campuses or engage in public controversies to defend
his tenaciously held position on the periphery. Most of all, he did
not seek or welcome disciples or imitators among the next gen-
eration of poets. Indeed, he had to view somewhat ironically the
steady succession of his published books as expressions of an ego
that needed, like all self-centered human egos, to be uncentered
from itself and absorbed in the brute beauty of inhuman nature
whose design is the godhead. On principle he willed himself to
oblivion.

As a result Jeffers is not much read or discussed today, although
encouraging indications of growing interest may initiate a reas-
sessment of his place in the pantheon of his extraordinary gen-

eration of poets. New editions of his work—*The Collected Poetry of Robinson Jeffers*, edited by Tim Hunt, 4 volumes (Stanford, Calif.: Stanford University Press, 1988–) and *Rock and Hawk: A Selection of Shorter Poems by Robinson Jeffers*, edited by Robert Hass (New York: Random House, Inc., 1987)—ought to bring Jeffers's poetry to a new and enlarged readership. At present, however, he is not much taught in courses on twentieth-century poetry; he is represented only perfunctorily in most anthologies and histories of the period; and there is no Jeffers tradition in American poetry, as there is a Whitman tradition, a Pound tradition, and an Eliot tradition. He had no poetic disciples or followers—except one. But that one is a remarkable and distinguished offspring.

William Everson was a moody, introspective young man for whom the San Joaquin town of Selma had provided little academic education, no career, no focus or channel for his restless mind and passionate spirit. In the fall of 1934, as a student at Fresno State, he chanced upon a volume of Jeffers's poetry in the library. That book broke upon him like a thunderclap, converting him to pantheism and confirming him in the poetic vocation. Almost immediately, Everson began to write the poems that over the years have made him, in my view, the most important California (or Western) poet after Jeffers.

They never met or corresponded; the one volume of his verse Everson sent Jeffers in filial recognition went unacknowledged. And other circumstances played their part in defining Everson's own voice and place in American letters: the influence of D. H. Lawrence; the years during the Second World War in a conscientious objectors' camp with other writers, artists, and printers; his association with Robert Duncan and Kenneth Rexroth after the war; and, most importantly, his conversion to Catholicism in 1949 and his almost twenty years as a Dominican lay brother under the name of Brother Antoninus, before his departure from the order in 1969. Nevertheless, Everson has remained loyal and devoted to Jeffers and in the process has become not only Jeffers's poetic disciple but one of the most knowledgeable scholars and critics of Jeffers. Everson's memorial poem for Jeffers, "The Poet Is Dead," is one of the most powerful elegies in American literature (it is included at the end of this book). His book of essays,

Robinson Jeffers: Fragments of an Older Fury, is a landmark critical study. He has edited for republication the double volume *Cawdor/ Medea*, *The Double Axe*, and Jeffers's youthful volume *Californians*; and from manuscript he has edited the previously unpublished poems in *The Alpine Christ* and *Brides of the South Wind*. As a master printer he designed a selection of Jeffers's poems about his house and tower under the title *Granite and Cypress*, which has been called one of the most magnificent books made by an American printer. And finally, Everson has served as a member of the editorial board for the Stanford edition of Jeffers's *Collected Poetry*.

All of which is a way of saying that *The Excesses of God*, Everson's study of Jeffers as a religious poet, is a most unusual and very special book, is itself, in fact, an event of literary distinction. Such a conjunction of two powerful poets does not occur often—especially not with such incandescence, illuminating not only their work and their connection but the deep strain of pantheistic mysticism in the American tradition as well. For if there is no Jeffers tradition, he clearly belongs to the autochthonous tradition that gives our expression its original and dominant character. So behind Jeffers stand Whitman and Jonathan Edwards, with Emerson and Thoreau as the pivot between them; after Jeffers come—besides Everson—Theodore Roethke, Gary Snyder, Allen Ginsberg, Wendell Berry, and Michael McClure. None of these writers shares Jeffers's Inhumanism, and the association among them is not at all simple or easy; indeed, the differences are as clarifying as the points of association. But in all there is a very American sense of location, an equally American commitment to organic nature as the energized ground of a revelation at once erotic and spiritual, and a consequent suspicion of ego-goals and civilization as subversive to the field of revelation.

This book is written as a series of overlapping and ever widening meditations on Jeffers's mysticism, on the sense of God, nature, self, and language informed and sustained by that mysticism; and these meditations take as text and illustration passages from Jeffers's poetry, some of the most extreme and overwhelming passages in our literature. Ultimately, the chapters have the integrity and the singularity of effect of a long essay. The prose itself emanates an argumentative vitality, sustained with a rhythmic measure and resonance that proceed from language drawing upon its deepest resources for orchestral articulation. Seldom is a critical book actually moving, intellectually as well as emotionally; this is one of those rare ones.

ALBERT GELPI

✦

Preface

This book was begun as the final chapter of a previous study, *Robinson Jeffers: Fragments of an Older Fury*, published under my religious name while I was still a member of the monastic community at Kentfield Priory, in Marin County, across the Golden Gate from San Francisco. It was not included in that book because my friend and publisher, Robert Hawley, pointed out that the chapter was too provisional and thin to serve the material under consideration.

"You have a book there rather than a mere chapter," he told me. "To be convincing, the equation you propose between Jeffers the poet and Otto the theologian has got to be more extensively developed, and presented in greater depth. Moreover, you ought to put more of yourself into it, draw on your own religious and poetic experience to give immediacy to the points you make. As both poet and monk, you are in a strong position to throw a third dimension into the duality of the other two voices, make the dialogue come alive from a fresh point of view." I was naturally disappointed that my chapter had not proved sufficient, but I took it back and went to work.

That was ten years ago. The admonition to put more of myself into the material proved easier said than done. The texts of Robinson Jeffers and Rudolph Otto flowed together naturally enough; but when it came to my own contribution, I found that a great deal of reflection was necessary—and beyond that, often a long wait for the given moment, the unpredictable instant when inspiration fused thought and feeling into spontaneous insight. Like poetry, this manuscript proved to be something I could not just pick up and work on at will.

So the years went by. I left the Dominican Order and in due course found myself involved in academic life. For many months at a time the book lay untouched, but other commitments to work on Jeffers always kept its issues close to my mind. My sense of its touching the central problem regarding him would not let me go. I was drawn back to it again and again, despite the creative effort it exacted.

Now, at last, it is completed. Begun in the monastery, finished in the world, its intermittent composition has left it sadly uneven. Still, I offer it as a testament to the genius of Robinson Jeffers, who for me still stands as the archetype of the spirit of this land—more brooding than Emerson, more sexual than Thoreau, more masculine and savage than Whitman, closer to the primordial spirit that lurks here—its violence, its jagged beauty, its terrifying immensity. But as for this work, if it has any merit, let the credit go to Bob Hawley, who denied me the easy issue of a chapter and drove me thereby to the ten years' birthpang of a book.

February 21, 1976   W. E.
Kresge College
University of California, Santa Cruz

As I returned to the above words, written just ten years ago, I found myself unable to account for the lapse of a decade since they were first set down. If the work were as close to completion as my Preface implies, what went awry?

As I recall, there remained only the final polishing of the last three chapters. But no, come to think of it, there was something more. As it happened, I was dissatisfied with the meditation opening the final chapter, "The Sex Element in the Religious Idea," and so I laid the work aside to await a better moment, just as I confessed to having done earlier. Finally, early this year, Bill Hotchkiss and Judith Shears offered to set up the work on their word processors, spurring me to action.

At last, after twenty long years, the book is done. Not that I am all that happy with the problematical meditation on sex and religion: as my favorite subject, it was to be a summing up, a cumulative effort of my lifelong reflection, but it proved disappointing. In the end, I went back to a version I had drafted several years ago because it is consistent in tone, says much that I mean, and errs largely in what it fails to say rather than what it attempts. I have learned to live with such insufficiencies.

To my old friends and compatriots, those who sustained me in the ordeal of this book across the years, once again I tender my deepest gratitude. They know who and what I mean, and I have not forgotten.

June 15, 1986   W. E.
Kingfisher Flat
Davenport, California

✦

Introduction

I. NO TOUR DE FORCE

On January 9, 1926, the day before Robinson Jeffers's thirty-ninth birthday, *The Monitor*, official newspaper of the Roman Catholic Archdiocese of San Francisco, printed the following editorial:

Pagan Horror from Carmel-by-the-Sea

Last Saturday the most widely circulated evening paper of San Francisco boasted that California has produced a great poet. Such matters must be met promptly by *The Monitor*.

Robinson Jeffers has the power of Aeschylus, the subtlety of Sophocles. Shelley and Swinburne played at being pagans. This is no tour de force. He is intrinsically terrible.

The first point to note is that he could not have produced such horror, had he not a pagan background in California and throughout America. Greater is our fright to note that our country has become so pagan as to produce such a writer. In college we read the Greek poets, but the Greek pagans were turned to dust. The modern pagans are alive.

The second point to note is to watch and pray. Some will accuse us of advertising Jeffers. He has already been advertised by papers shamefully read in Catholic homes. This is a warning to watch and prevent our children from having their souls scarred by the reading of this modern pagan giant's corruption. This is not a matter of preventing curiosity but of saving them from a devastating decadence.[1]

Jeffers's bibliographer, S. S. Alberts, in reprinting this item, refers to it as an "admonitory philippic,"[2] but that word hardly does it justice. Certainly it is a good deal more than admonitory. And were it only a philippic, the editorialist would have cried for the book's suppression. But obviously he is shaken. Too stunned for shrill denunciation, the man is genuinely appalled.

I introduce the matter, more or less as an anecdote, in order to underscore the fact that as I began this book in January of 1966, just forty years after *The Monitor* sounded its alarm, a Jesuit priest at the University of San Francisco gained his doctorate with a dissertation entitled "Symbolic Themes in the Poetry of Robinson Jeffers," a devout Catholic laywoman was editing his *Collected Letters*; a Catholic graduate student at Kenyon College was writing his thesis on "The Philosophy of Robinson Jeffers," and I, a Dominican lay brother, was correcting proof on my first study of the poet.[3] How many nuns there were busily researching the *Selected Poetry* for themes I could not know, but it would have been imprudent to assume that none existed. Anyone seriously concerned with the temper of religion in America sooner or later confronts this giant and acknowledges his force.

For the power that forty years ago shook *The Monitor* as sheer unmitigated paganism is the same power that eight years later broke my own acquired agnosticism and compelled me to think of myself as a manifestly religious man. It is a power I still attest to in writing this study, a power that I continue to regard as an undiluted religious force. *The Monitor's* editorial, nominally an instance of clerical hostility to unbridled genius or freedom in the arts, is actually an attestation that, from the beginning, Jeffers's work struck through to the religious dimension, and with a power that has been particularly felt by those who know what religion is. "This is no tour de force. The man is intrinsically terrible." It is the way that I, too, felt about Jeffers when I first read him. It is what gripped me, stopped me in my tracks, and changed my life. That it seemed paganism to the twenties is hardly surprising—the themes *are* horrendous—but that, transcending the themes, the vision of God in which the themes are cast is awesome and worshipful, is today apparent. It can, in fact, no longer be questioned.

I propose, therefore, to treat Jeffers as a religious figure. In so doing I will not have recourse to his philosophy. As a matter of fact, it seems to me that one of the chief benefits deriving from such a perspective is precisely to shift the point of emphasis away from his philosophical content. The recent works on Jeffers have dealt largely with his speculative thought, seeking to find therein the key to his place in contemporary letters. The central body of Mercedes Monjian's book, for instance, is divided into two sections, "The Philosopher-Poet" and "The Poet-Philosopher."[4]

Radcliffe Squires's work centers chiefly on Jeffers as a philosopher, with chapters on Nietzsche, Schopenhauer, Spengler, Whitman, and Lucretius.[5] And while Frederic Carpenter observes that "the religious nature of Jeffers' poetry has not been sufficiently recognized," his prior observation that "more completely than any other modern American, Jeffers is a philosophical poet," indicates the point at which the thought rather than the mystical content of the poems is stressed.[6] More recently Robert J. Brophy's work has thrown the emphasis toward the mystical structure in Jeffers's poetry, and Bill Hotchkiss has investigated his centrality to the traditional aesthetic consensus, but it is safe to say that the formal reflection on Jeffers's performance since he began to write has been concentrated largely around philosophical interests, what might be called "the burden of his thought."[7]

Yet something more, something other, always remains to be said, as if the weight of philosophical emphasis still leaves us with a mystery, a great question mark concerning the man. Lucretius or Schopenhauer, Nietzsche or Spengler—they have their bearing points, indeed, but none of them, nor any combination of them, suffices to put our minds at rest about him: philosophically everything leads to the impasse of his monumental contradictions. Something in him is always breaking beyond and below the speculative content. The strands of his philosophical thought approach each other but never meet. Considered primarily as philosophical poetry, the edifice of his achievement remains without resolution. Something refuses to jell.

I think this is so because Jeffers is not, actually, a philosophical poet at all. He certainly has recourse to philosophy, just as he certainly has recourse to science, but the attempt to categorize him as a philosopher will remain as unsatisfactory as would a similar attempt to categorize him as a scientist. In fact, more might be said for him as a scientific poet than as a philosophical one, for Hyatt Howe Waggoner draws an antipathetical sketch that rings with a certain relevance:

If any have supposed that Robinson's fears, Frost's scoffing, and Eliot's disdainful turning of the back on modernism and the implications of science were without any justification, there is the work of Mr. Jeffers, for-

mer student of medicine, brother of an astronomer, frequent visitor to
observatories, and constant reader of scientific books and journals, to
correct them. Mr. Jeffers is in a position to know what the implications
of science are for the status of values. I believe a deeper knowledge of
modern science and scientific philosophy than most literary critics have
would show that he does know, though his information does not seem
to be the latest available. He is the only modern poet whose work is
widely held to be important who has accepted without any qualification
the views of life and man explicitly offered or implicitly suggested by the
traditional scientific texts.[8]

My purpose, then, is to shift the focus away from the approach
accented in recent years, to do this by regarding Jeffers not as a
philosophical poet but as a religious one, and, moreover, not as
a religious *thinker* who, in the manner of Dante, uses poetry as
his theological vehicle, but rather one who stands religiously
committed not on the basis of thought but of attitude, a disposi-
tion primarily and consistently of the heart and only secondarily
and inconsistently of the mind.

In order to do this, it is necessary to go not to the source of his
thought but to the source of his feeling—to explore the implica-
tions of Carpenter's observation that "the apparent exaggera-
tions and inconsistencies of Jeffers' philosophy sometimes have
their roots in a religious feeling older than philosophy itself."[9]
And it will permit us to understand the power of the only real
unity that Monjian, having denied him unity of form and unity
of thought, accords him: unity of mood. "Here Jeffers is a mas-
ter. . . . Through this depressing convergence of image, setting,
subject, and tone, Jeffers comes closest to achieving his purpose,
and we begin to believe that 'we must uncenter our minds from
ourselves' to escape catastrophe."[10]

Braced against the unrelenting didacticism of his thought, we
must shift our gaze to the omnipresence of religious feeling that
floods his verse. Thus readjusted, let us see if this approach ad-
mits of any structuring process that will enable us to assent con-
clusively to its primacy, since the philosophical approach refuses
to yield to any such conclusion. Whether or not it does, the find-
ings of such a study should at least let us get his thought a little
more in focus—give us, that is, a bit more comprehension of what
he is talking about.

II. THE IDEA OF THE HOLY

Today we take for granted a working distinction between the institutional and the charismatic factors in religious experience, but fifty years ago the matter had to be insisted upon. Religious life in America was, by and large, solidly institutional, and most irregular charismatic attempts, whether the proliferation of evangelical sects, or the go-it-alone religious solitary of the backwoods or the ghetto, had to bear the full opprobrium of the charge of "enthusiasm."

But when I came to write this book in the late 1960's, the situation was exactly reversed. Religious institutionalism, true, had survived the overwhelming onslaught of world revolution, reductive Freudian skepticism, and the universal triumph of secularism. Its social and political force, as registered in sheer mass power, remained impressive, but it was everywhere on the defensive.

Conversely, the prestige of unstructured charismatic religious experience was phenomenal: under no necessity to justify itself, it actually presumed to define the primary moral and spiritual posture. The hippies, its self-appointed advocates, arrogated to themselves a kind of judiciary of the unconscious, inexorably judging, by their relaxed stance, the rest of humanity, while coolly disclaiming judgment altogether.

A succession of movements and fads, from Vedanta immediately after World War II, to Zen Buddhism in the following decade, led the growing preoccupation with high states of consciousness, until it became impossible to predict which way or how far the trend would go. Psychedelic proponents claimed to have swept away the old laborious mystical ascesis. The classic "preparation for vision" involving prayer, fasting, penitential practices, all designed to modify thought processes sequentially and effect a gradual displacement of consciousness, was instead undertaken by a carefully spaced administration of the particular drug. The historic transition from Novice to Proficient to Adept was said to be accomplished virtually overnight by the progression from marijuana to peyote to lysergic acid. Instant mysticism had arrived. Before the court of law the hippies demanded freedom for LSD the way the early Christians demanded freedom for the Eucharist.

One of the chief texts that accomplished this revolution in attitude, this authentification of naked religious sensibility, was Rudolf Otto's *The Idea of the Holy*. It was published in 1917, during the terrible war that accomplished, through fearful purgation, Jeffers's own religious revision, though it is unlikely that he ever read the book. When we turn away from Christianity or any other form of absolute belief, we generally turn with a clenched heart, and want nothing further to do with the creed we feel has failed us. Very likely Otto would have interested Jeffers only mildly if at all. Within a few years, with the fixity of the truly obsessed, he would be hewing out his own vision, scarcely to be inveigled by the nuances of traditional affective states of mind.

But in *The Idea of the Holy*, Otto sought to restore some of the elemental vitality Jeffers abandoned Christianity to find. He sought to sweep away the speculative and ethical superstructure that had grown over the roots of religious experience itself, and which depth psychology was beginning to rediscover in the unconscious, delving down to the basic responses that characterize primordial religious feeling (Jung's *Symbols of Transformation*, for example, was published in 1912). Otto sought, principally, to demarcate those aspects of religious immediacy which such words as *holiness* cannot accommodate, recognizing that in advanced Christian cultures they had been totally appropriated by the concept "good," in the moral and ethical sense, while something more basic, more primitive and elemental, shrank away and disappeared. He writes:

The fact is that we have come to use the words "holy" and "sacred" in an entirely derivative sense, quite different from that which they originally bore. We generally take "holy" as meaning "completely good": it is the absolute moral attribute, denoting the consummation of moral goodness. In this sense Kant calls the will which remains unwaveringly obedient to the moral law from the motive of duty a "holy will"; here clearly we have simply the *perfectly moral* will.[11]

But Otto protested that such usage denies too much. "It is true that all this moral significance is contained in the word 'holy,' but it includes in addition—as even we cannot but feel—a clear over-

plus of meaning, and this is now our task to isolate."[12] Otto
pointed out that such an overplus was actually the original de-
posit of the word, and in order to establish what that overplus is,
he sought to invent a special term to stand for "the holy" *minus
its moral factor* and its "rational" content altogether.

For this purpose I adopt a word from the Latin, *numen*. *Omen* has given
us "ominous," and there is no reason why from *numen* we should not
similarly form a word "numinous." I shall speak, then, of a unique "nu-
minous" category of value and of a definitely "numinous" state of mind,
which is always found wherever the category is applied. This mental
state is perfectly *sui generis* and irreducible to any other; and therefore,
like every absolutely primary and elemental datum, while it admits of
being discussed, it cannot be strictly defined.[13]

Rather it can only be suggested by means of the special way in
which it is reflected in the mind, identifiable only in terms of feel-
ing. "Its nature is such that it grips or stirs the human mind with
this and that affective state."[14]

In the years since Otto wrote, his term has been universally
adopted, not only in theological writing, but in the vocabulary of
psychological and symbolic analysis as well, becoming, in fact,
one of our key verbal tools for designating religious, or awe-
struck, states of mind. It is the term I shall chiefly rely on in dis-
cussing Jeffers as a religious poet because, more than any other,
the feeling that he himself most consciously cultivates is the
sense of the numinous when apprehended directly in nature.
Poets, of course, generally evoke it as authentic mystery; I do not
hesitate to acknowledge Jeffers a religious poet because he evokes
it unequivocally as God.

In translating this universally perceived numen back into the
divine, Mircea Eliade cites Otto's work to introduce his own par-
ticular refinements. In a chapter entitled "Power and Holiness,"
from his book *Myths, Dreams, and Mysteries*, he acknowledges Ot-
to's priority and offers a corresponding term, which serves to lo-
calize the numinous in its specifying form of self-disclosure or
revelation:

The sacred, then, manifests itself equally as a force or as a power. To de-
note the act of manifestation of the sacred, we propose to use the term

hierophany. This word is convenient because it requires no additional specification; it means nothing more than is implied by its etymological content—namely, that something sacred is shown to us, manifests itself.[15]

Then he proceeds to specify the universal character behind the entire phenomenon, having already noted that language, being analogical, "is obliged to try to suggest whatever surpasses natural experience in terms that are borrowed from that experience." He goes on:

One may say that the history of religions—from the most elementary to the most developed—is constituted by a number of important hierophanies, manifestations of sacred realities. Beginning from the most elementary hierophany—for example, the manifestation of the sacred in any object whatever, say a stone or a tree—and ending in the supreme hierophany, the incarnation of God in Jesus Christ, there is no real break in the continuity.[16]

His conclusion is:

This is most important for our understanding of the specific character of religious experience: if we admit that all manifestations of the sacred are equivalent as such, in that the humblest hierophany and the most terrifying theophany present the same structure and are to be explained by the same dialectic of the sacred, we then realize that there is no essential discontinuity in the religious life of mankind.[17]

It is within such a context that the sacred vision of Robinson Jeffers may serve to revivify our modern religious sensibilities. Within this fundamental equation, the effort in this study will be to restore, through that vision, something of the power and the grandeur that the authentic religious poets, from all ages and from all creeds, have given back to the race.

+

ONE

+

All Flesh Is Grass

+

The voice said, Cry.
And he said, What shall I cry?
All flesh is grass,
And all the goodliness thereof
Is as the flower of the fields: . . .
Surely the people is grass.
The grass withereth, the flower fadeth:
But the word of our God shall stand forever.

Isaiah 40: 6–8

✦

I. CREATURE-CONSCIOUSNESS

"The satisfaction that men take in evidences of the life of nature and its power, and above all in surpassing manifestations of that power, is one of the perennial roots of religion." With these words Amos Wilder opens his chapter on "The Nihilism of Mr. Robinson Jeffers" in *The Spiritual Aspects of the New Poetry*.[1]

If Jeffers ever read this book, it could not have pleased him, for he knew himself to be no nihilist, or one only in a very highly qualified and extended sense. But one part of the chapter must have given him delight. Wilder quotes from a scientist's report, *The Vesuvius Eruption of 1906: Study of a Volcanic Cycle*, written by a student of volcanic phenomena, Dr. Frank A. Perret. As Wilder presents the text in his extended quote, it is a fitting introduction to the central feature of our study:

Strongest of all impressions received in the course of these remarkable events, greatest of all surprises . . . was, for the writer, that of an infinite dignity in every manifestation of this stupendous releasing of energy. No words can describe the majesty of its unfolding, the utter absence of anything resembling effort, and the all-sufficient power to perform the allotted task and to do it majestically. Each rapid impulse was the crest of something deep and powerful and uniform which bore it, and the unhurried modulation of its rhythmic beats sets this eruption in the rank of things which are mighty, grave and great.

There was present also the element of awe, in all its fullness. The phenomena entered, through their intensity, that sphere where the normal conditions of Nature are overpassed, and one stands in the presence of greater and more elemental forces than any he has known hitherto. This tends to induce a state of mind which hardly recognizes as entirely natural this transformation of the visible universe, and with difficulty one accepts the dictum of reason, that all will pass and the normal return as before; and so, for the many, the events of this and the succeeding days of ashy darkness seemed to show that—even as the younger Pliny wrote of similar conditions in this same region nearly two thousand years ago—"the last eternal night of story has settled on the world."

But it is precisely this projection beyond the borderland of the obvious which gives to such events their majesty—the dignity which, allied with the mysterious, is thereby perfected. The sense-walls of the Universe are shattered by these higher values of power, and Deity is indirectly more in evidence than in the case of the lesser things. A blade of grass as surely, but far less forcibly, reveals the truth that That which manifests cannot be seen, nor heard, nor felt, except through and because of the manifestation.[2]

This passage could have been written by Jeffers himself, though the deity is but mentioned. The poet would have *invoked* him.

It is a commonplace of philosophical psychology that there can be no conception in the mind which has not been based upon a prior sense impression in the body. From this it follows that the priority of the image, the image which precedes mentality, endows the religious spirit with the plenitude of its material forms. The ordinary man sees God in Nature or he sees Him not at all. By extension, the God-thirsting man sees Him everywhere, for Nature is omnipresent. Moreover, Nature's manifold forms shimmer and glow with an intense vibration, the rudimentary abstract that gives them the universal character of existence. Both sides tend to endow the substance of tangible things—against which the claims of pure transcendence are always shattering—with the ineradicable impress of divinity. Thus even the system of Plotinus, "than which," in the words of the *Encyclopedia Americana*, "nothing is more opposed to pantheism," collapses into absorption, making as it does of God "so pure an abstraction that even thought, without being separated from individuality, cannot attain to it." For "even from the bosom of this school a prolific source of pantheism was born."[3]

The poet exults. Stunned by the impact of spontaneous wholeness revealed everywhere about him, he manifests the words that will clue its essence, not at all intimidated by Eliade's dictum that "language, being analogical, is obliged to suggest whatever surpasses natural experience in terms that are borrowed from that experience." Born of the experience rather than borrowed from it, his speech bears the impress of the same vibration, achieves consonance with the sum of things, registers wholeness through the relevance of utterance. What is uttered is established, exists of the phenomenon that evoked it. Emerson said that nature is the language of God. It is fittingly spoken, for "in the beginning was the

Word." And in that beginning is its end. The Word, then, is all. For Nature itself holds the clue to the divine. In its myriad forms, the great plenitude of being is poured out, streaming from the womb of potentiality, exploding into act. A kind of metaphysical combustion seems smoldering in the fabric of things, a surge of incipient energy, breaking out of the bounds of its nuclear forms, and disappearing into the beyond. It is this transformation the poet celebrates.

Gazing about him with an enravished eye, he becomes the menstruum through which the presence of things achieves participation in the world of the abstract, the dimension of mind. The word sings. Stimulus and response are one; they are the quintessential divinities sealed in the multiplicity of shapes: "The signature of all things." In the web of transcendent words, the poet fuses potency and act. For the poet, potentiality is the domain of his sovereignty, not as between cause and effect, but as between corresponding identities. But it is from act to potentiality that he emerges as the preceptor of unity—the pure pantheist.

For wherever he looks, the scale and vastness present to the poet simply the correspondences of what he is, plunging back from act to potentiality, to realize the mystery of inchoation. His sovereign authority is this investiture in the common substance of coexistence. His mind dazzles with mutuality, but his spirit is cool with a searching recognition, knowledge gazing at its own preknowledge, the four eyes of comprehension absorbed in the synthesis where nothing divides. The hierarchies of being fade before the universality of the contingent, the degree that subsumes in his expression. His godlike thirst is sourced in his propensity, the sovereign seizure of the Word. Language for him is the divine abyss. Out of it float and emerge the shapes of unconceived essences. What he utters is greater than what he intuits, and this is his sinecure within the criteria of value. He gives back to the world, to the common mind, the coeval images of its own existence. His declaration "I speak truth" is no lie.

Then where resides his humility? What becomes of his creaturehood? His creaturehood is the marginal condition lurking at the corners of his failure. Unable to sustain manifestation, he slumps back into the contingent. Correspondences elude him. He mumbles the formulae of sentient approximation. The mun-

dane substance of measurable observance, the scrutinies of ob-
served distinction, clot his lips. And in the trap of the contingent,
he merely babbles. "The poets lie too much." Gazing through the
lens of the learned astronomer, he exclaims like any journalist,
marveling at the distances that separate mote from mote. From
the pure pantheist of ineluctable transcendence, he becomes the
philosophical pantheist of empirical immanence. His tongue is
shut. He has reentered history, and he has become no more than
its most imaginative expresser. When he fails his vocation, he be-
comes its slave.

In the cultural dethronement, following Galileo, of what Eliade
termed "the supreme hierophany, the incarnation of God in Jesus
Christ,"[4] it inevitably came about that the cosmos itself assumed
the aspects of the divine, but not in the sense of mere comparison.
In that crisis of intellectual consciousness which we call the Co-
pernican revolution, the substitutive natural hierophany that
supplanted Christ could be nothing less than the Immensity it-
self. Philosophical pantheism—the substitutive religion that pre-
vailed between Copernicus, who rendered incarnation obsolete,
and Einstein, who restored it to feasibility—has somehow always
been associated with the development of astronomy.

For if it is physics which analyzes the substance of the cosmos,
it is astronomy which measures its scale. More than any other sci-
ence, it is astronomy which presents to the intellect the config-
uration of the cosmos itself. And it is in the configuration, the
image, that man's intellect, in the deeps of its residual cognition,
discerns its God.

Thus, at the decline of Rome, it was the development of Syrian
astrology that gave the mystery cults invading the empire on
every side the force to produce the intellectual climate in which
Neoplatonism was transmuted from gnosticism to pantheism.
Again it was the development of astronomy following Galileo
that gave the pantheistic insights of Bruno and Spinoza their force
in men's thought. For as the skeptical spirit, in its conquest of
space and time, canceled out the efflux of the divine by reducing
the numinous, or awesome, to the principle of mere material
cause-and-effect, that spirit nevertheless could not refrain from
stretching upward and outward in search of the source of awe in

the terminal limits that define each dimension: the place Mystery lurks. And when, with the advance of cognizance in the wake of the advance of astronomy, it expands with the illimitable cosmos, the mind itself tingles on inchoation, and the numinous awe it was busily canceling out in the search for pure objectivity—devouring all hierophanies up from sacred stone and sacred tree to the divine Jesus Himself—when that awe overwhelms the mind with sheer vastness, and its concomitant, sheer duration, then a greater awe returns upon it than any particular hierophany could wring from its depth. Although the mind could nowhere bow to the individual symptom, the particular hierophany, it suddenly finds itself on its knees before the archetype of every hierophany, namely the All. Thus a perennial contradiction is reborn.

For, as the *Catholic Encyclopedia* puts it, "to a thoroughgoing pantheist there can be no creaturehood. All is all. This contradiction falls into place because even philosophically pantheism is not so much a doctrine as it is an attitude, the implication of views expressed in terms of the world, God, the Absolute, or Infinity. What it does is to emphasize the immanence of God in the world and de-emphasize or ignore His transcendence over the world."[5]

Thus Jeffers can say: "Another theme that has engaged my verses is the expression of a religious feeling, that perhaps must be called pantheism, though I hate to type it with a name. It is the feeling—I will say the certainty—that the universe is one being, a single organism, one great life that includes all life and all things; and is so beautiful that it must be loved and reverenced; and in moments of mystical vision we identify ourselves with it."[6] So said the poet, with his philosophical back to the wall, when compelled to defend his position.

If he is not absolutely consistent in the various attestations to be found in his verse, it is no wonder. "For since," continues the *Catholic Encyclopedia*, "no philosopher has as yet failed to make some distinction between the transcendent and immanent aspects of divine being, there never has been a complete and utter pantheism."[7]

This is unequivocally stated, but returning to the *Encyclopedia Americana* we find the same tone, if not the same words. The historians of ideas, regardless of dogmatic adherence, boil down their subjects into the most terse formulae. Here it says of pantheism: "The doctrine stands midway between atheism and dogmatic theism" and goes on to observe: "The origin of the idea of a God with the theist and the pantheist is the same. It is by reasoning upon ourselves and the surrounding objects of which we are cognizant that we come to infer the existence of some Superior Being upon whom they all depend, from whom they proceed or in whom they subsist. Pantheism assumed the identity of cause and effect, and the consequent adequacy of each effect, rightly interpreted, to indicate its cause."[8] It is for this reason that I called the poet, in the throes of his creative vision, the pure pantheist—because in the deeps of the creative intuition, that is the way he sees reality. But the vision is unsustainable, and when he slumps back into creaturehood, his tongue falters.

Now the poetic vision, although an illuminative state, does not exist in isolation because, invested in language, it proceeds by two channels, the channels of thought and feeling. The poet can only ascend to vision by virtue of them, and when he descends from vision, these remain, like filaments in a light bulb, not incandescent but nevertheless there. It is thus no accident that our study is not destined to treat of Jeffers the poet *per se*; it will not be a selection and analysis of his best passages. Nor will it, as we have said, treat of his thought, which has already found so much attention. Rather, it will focus upon his feelings, and it defines him as a religious poet by virtue of their predominantly religious character. But we have only to glance at his verse to be aware at the outset that this feeling-content projects us into a contradiction with his thought, a contradiction which he resolved in what we can only call his cosmic vision.

To a degree this is, of course, true of every poet: once we have retired from the domain of the unifying vision, the upper register that transcends distinctions, we are back in the inferior categories of thought and feeling. And when it comes to Jeffers, we encounter as radical a difference between them as we expect to find in someone of complex and agonized sensibility. The son of a clergyman, he naturally began as a theist, and it was here that all his feeling-responses took shape. His thought came later, much later. An intensive scientific training must have confronted him with the atheistic premises, the dominant alternative to the theistic impress of his formation, so that between them his pantheism emerged to provide a resolution for the intellectual split common to his time and culture. Although his scientific education led him to *think* in terms of a God of immanence, his deep religious sensibility could only decree that he *feel* in terms of a God of transcendence. It is this latter voice that we are exploring in our study, and it is everywhere evident. Time and again in his poetry he is brought to his knees, as it were, before the recognition of a God so vast, so overwhelming, so infinitely beyond all the discernible manifestations of the concrete, that every syllable he utters suggests, above the voice by which he speaks them, the implications of his awe: "I am nothing." It is with this cry that we can begin our investigation of the work of Jeffers as it applies to Rudolf Otto and the Idea of the Holy.

Otto posits as the very basis of that idea a state of being which he can only categorize "creature-consciousness," or "creature-feeling"—the emotion, he says, of a creature submerged and overwhelmed by its own nothingness, a nullity of self realized in contrast to that which is infinitely beyond it, to a being inexpressibly supreme above all creatures. Furthermore, he rejects any attempt to conceptualize it. All that his term creature-feeling can express, he insists, is the note of a submergence into nothingness before an overpowering, absolute might, a total, annihilative force. "Everything turns upon the *character* of this overpowering might, a character which cannot be expressed verbally, and can only be suggested indirectly through the tone and content of a man's feeling-response to it. And this response must be directly experienced in oneself to be understood."[9] As an instance he notes Abraham's self-abnegating cry after pleading on behalf of the men of Sodom: "Behold now, I have taken upon me to speak unto the Lord, which am but dust and ashes."[10] And in correspondence to this, one remembers Job's effacement of all he is before the Lord's absoluteness: "Behold, I am vile. What shall I answer thee? I will lay mine hand upon my mouth."[11]

But Otto takes care to insist that this feeling, for all its depth of interiority, is no mere subjective state. Rather, the creature-feeling is itself a manifestation of quite another psychic component, an element which, he says, by its nature is denotative of something beyond, an objective recognition of the existence of what is radically other than, and infinitely superior to, the experiencing self. No mere subjective state can engender self-inferiority. The self cannot feel inferior to itself. What it can feel is its vulnerability before that which it recognizes as imponderably greater than it, that which can overwhelm and annihilate it. Out of this recognition religion itself is born. And because of it religion can be affirmed as a true, rather than an evasive response to the self's travail in its ordeal of existence.

However, this objective recognition of cosmic inferiority stands as polar opposite to the self's counter-knowledge, its corresponding intuition of superiority upon which secularism, as distinct from the religious attitude, is founded. For such is the superiority of the human intellect to the material categories of being around us that we not unnaturally relate from a position of advantage, eschewing the disadvantage of a self-effacing inferiority to that which transcends us. What is natural and easy becomes habitual and reflexive, and as success follows success in its conquest of the phenomenal world, the self, turning inward, becomes preoccupied with its own discriminations and in time exalts itself by diverting all its energies to its byplay of instigation and control.

Following this, civilization and then culture erect a context of interreactive congratulatory ritualism, a preoccupation which thoroughly indoctrinates every nascent generation until, in time, a veritable haze of deceptive self-consciousness hangs over all man's activity. Religion itself partakes of it, and though indispensable, the weakness or defective side of that very indispensability is precisely its tendency to augment, by repetition and custom, the glare of self-preoccupation, of self-absorption, which covers all man's thought. Although theology can conceptualize human inferiority to God, conceptualization cannot produce the creature-feeling, the shuddering realization of self-effacement and nullity in which that recognition must achieve finality. When religion shirks or flees from this painful necessity, it becomes (by a kind of hideous reversal of functions) itself the primary vehicle of human pride. Our corruption is complete.

It is specifically against this deceptive complacency, this blind presumption of collective human sufficiency, that Jeffers directs the holy violence of his utterance. And he does it not by reference to higher and higher categories of psychic and spiritual perception, which is the gnostic's feature, but by a brusque shift of emphasis back toward "inferior" categories, the world of material phenomena and processes. For he intuits that it is precisely in these categories and objects that the numinous now obtains: it is precisely by considering humanity from a point of view *below* these categories that the all-important creature-feeling may be restored to him, that he can at last see himself as he is, as his basic situation in existence proclaims him to be.

Jeffers's most obvious technique in securing this fundamental transferral of attitude, this shift from deceptive superiority to realistic inferiority, is that of reduction. Although his work continually implies such devaluation by its tone, often enough he breaks out in direct statement, inverting the vaunted domain of man to minuscule proportions. For instance, in "Apology for Bad Dreams," he depicts an outrageous act, a woman and her son torturing a horse, which is itself, by definition, subhuman. Then, drawing perspective above it with increasing elevation, he secures, through an inexorable reduction, this processive devaluation of man within the grandeur of the cosmos he inhabits:

Seen from this height they are shrunk to insect size.
Out of all human relation. You cannot distinguish
The blood dripping from where the chain is fastened,
The beast shuddering; but the thrust neck and the legs
Far apart. You can see the whip fall on the flanks . . .
The gesture of the arm. You cannot see the face of the woman.
The enormous light beats up out of the west across the cloudbars of
   the trade-wind. The ocean
Darkens, the high clouds brighten, the hills darken together.
   Unbridled and unbelievable beauty
Covers the evening world . . . not covers, grows apparent out of it[12]

Sometimes the reduction is not the sustained diminution of receding vision and heightening consciousness, but rather is fleetingly glimpsed, a glance in passing, one momentary insight into the essential transience of earth's most permanent fixtures, its most basic proportional diminutions, as in this passage from "Mara":

He found himself for a lightning moment
Outside the flux and whirl of things, observing the world
From a fixed point. He saw the small spinning planet,
Spotted with white at the poles and dull red wars

Branding both cheeks, and the sun and the other stars like a herd of
        wild horses
On the vast field, but all vanished with the lightning[13]

    And sometimes the uses of reduction are applied not only to
size and quantity but to life-processes themselves. These are tele-
scoped together, as in the vision of the archetypal eagle in *Cawdor*.
The great captive bird, dispatched out of mercy, strips bondage
in a mighty leap of death and soars:

                    This rose,
Possessing the air over its emptied prison,
The eager powers at its shoulders waving shadowless
Unwound the ever-widened spirals of flight
As a star light, it spins the night-stabbing threads
From its own strength and substance: so the aquiline desire
Burned itself into meteor freedom and spired
Higher still, and saw the mountain-dividing
Canyon of its captivity (that was to Cawdor
Almost his world) like an old crack in a wall,
Violet-shadowed and gold-lighted; the little stain
Spilt on the floor of the crack was the strong forest;
The grain of sand was the Rock. A speck, an atomic
Center of power clouded in its own smoke
Ran and cried in the crack; it was Cawdor; the other
Points of humanity had neither weight nor shining
To prick the eyes of even an eagle's passion.[14]

Man is infinitesimally reduced, but Jeffers cannot abide at this
level. The reduction continues in the eagle's inexorable ascent:

This burned and soared. The shining ocean below lay on the shore
Like the great shield of the moon come down, rolling bright rim to rim
        with the earth. Against it the multiform
And many-canyoned coast-range hills were gathered into one carven
        mountain, one modulated
Eagle's cry made stone, stopping the strength of the sea. The beaked
        and winged effluence
Felt the air foam under its throat and saw
The mountain sun-cup Tassajara, where fawns
Dance in the steam of the hot fountains at dawn,
Smoothed out, and the high strained ridges beyond Cachagua,
Where the rivers are born and the last condor is dead,
Flatten, and a hundred miles toward morning the Sierras

Dawn with their peaks of snow, and dwindle and smooth down
On the globed earth.[15]

The imagery has become at once more symbolic and more rare-
fied, as the height increases, but the moral is not lessened, the
application remains human:

> It saw from the height and desert space of unbreathable air
> Where meteors make green fire and die, the oceans dropping
>   westward to the girdle of the pearls of dawn
> And the hinder edge of the night sliding toward Asia; it saw far under
>   eastward the April-delighted
> Continent; and time relaxing about it now, abstracted from being, it
>   saw the eagles destroyed,
> Mean generations of gulls and crows taking their world: turn for turn
>   in the air, as on earth
> The white faces drove out the brown. It saw the white decayed and the
>   brown from Asia returning;
> It saw men learn to outfly the hawk's brood and forget it again; it saw
>   men cover the earth and again
> Devour each other and hide in caverns, be scarce as wolves. It neither
>   wondered nor cared, and it saw
> Growth and decay alternate forever, and the tides returning.[16]

Sometimes the reductive device is positioned from a terminal
stasis, the very fixity adding, in contrast to the momentary
glimpse, or the telescoped process, an almost pitilessly unwav-
ering finality of judgment, as in this passage from "The Broken
Balance":

> I remember the farther
> Future, and the last man dying
> Without succession under the confident eyes of the stars.
> It was only a moment's accident,
> The race that plagued us; the world resumes the old lonely immortal
> Splendor; from here I can even
> Perceive that that snuffed candle had something . . . a fantastic virtue,
> A faint and unshapely pathos . . .
> So death will flatter them at last: what, even the bald ape's by-shot
> Was moderately admirable?[17]

But the registration of creature-feeling, while it may employ
them, is never dependent upon such objective devices for its
presence in the poem. More often it manifests itself in the deeper

sense that Otto means, a profound affective condition of awed awareness. It is as if Jeffers's imagination is in a perpetual state of tenuousness before the vastness of things, and it is this acute apprehension which must account for his obsession with permanence, and the valuation of phenomena that are less changeful than flesh. Secular mentalities, irked by what seems almost a perverseness, seek out flaws in the logic, or resort to semantic quarreling, to indict his trend. But the religious mind understands well enough that these permanences which obsess him are operating as symbols, abiding points on which to found the deeper consciousness, and are clues to the dark core of the creature-feeling that shapes the human undercast of anxiety.

For the reductive devices we have instanced here have, as such, their obvious limitations. Though dramatic, and convenient to categorize, they cannot of necessity occur with any very great frequency; otherwise, like all devices, they become increasingly tedious and cancel themselves out. The greater thing, the unconscious bodying-forth of the feeling-response, occurs more pervasively and more subtly in the palpable lyrics. These epiphanies of religious awareness would be more fruitful to explore, but the larger prospect must here occupy us, involving though it does an inevitable simplification. But before going on to specific details, it must be emphasized that everything Jeffers wrote was touched by his acute awareness of this underlying disparity between the human ego and the greater reality it fails to contemplate, an awareness that constitutes the principal factor by which we recognize him as an essentially religious poet.

"Autumn Evening," taken almost at random from among dozens of poems, must serve for example. Here the creature-feeling colors but does not obtrude. Explicitly attested in no more than the turning of a phrase, it nonetheless suffuses the whole before the poem closes and is let go by. Note how the so-called pathetic fallacy, largely deemed a liability by critical opinion, is here potent, powerfully evoking the felt experience:

> Though the little clouds ran southward still, the quiet autumnal
> Cool of the late September evening
> Seemed promising rain, rain, the change of the year, the angel
> Of the sad forest. A heron flew over
> With that remote ridiculous cry, "Quawk," the cry

That seems to make silence more silent. A dozen
Flops of the wing, a drooping glide, at the end of the glide
The cry, and a dozen flops of the wing.
I watched him pass on the autumn-colored sky; beyond him
Jupiter shone for evening star.
The sea's voice worked into my mood, I thought "No matter
What happens to men . . . the world's well made though."[18]

The choice idiomatic pungency suddenly reveals the underlying
irreconcilability between the human and the divine in the reli-
gious heart of the poet. Man is restored to his creaturehood: he
looks again upon his world with awe.

II. MYSTERIUM TREMENDUM

Of all man's experiences, the awareness of God is his most fun-
damental and, by a kind of maddening contradiction, his most
intangible and incommunicable. Back at the beginning, it must
have been this first awareness that brought home to him the dis-
quieting isolateness that set him off from the brutes. For what nat-
ural propensity does he possess but some animal he knows of ex-
cels him in its exercise? Not sexual transport, certainly. There are
in his range of experience several species that he cannot hope to
equal in the physical ecstasy with which they couple. Not in pa-
rental devotion. The sow grizzly displays an unfailing capacity
for self-sacrifice on behalf of her young that no woman can equal.
Not in nuptual fidelity. Canada geese mate once and, if death sev-
ers the union, remain single to the end. Not in hunger for home.
The pigeon returns unerringly to its nest, and the salmon seeks
the headwaters of its spawn in order to reproduce itself in the ma-
trix of its origins.

And so it goes. Wherever we look, some animal (as by a special
faculty) exceeds us in an exercise of virtue we unreflectingly re-
garded as our own. We tacitly acknowledge this by symbolizing
our most esteemed propensities under specific forms of animal
life: the lion for courage, the dog for devotion, the serpent for
cunning. Civilized man, reaching higher, places that superiority
in his capacity to entertain abstractions, his gift for abstract
thought, and this is correct. But long before he could promulgate

elementary equations, he must have been aware of this intuitional distinction as an experience of the reality of God, a special faculty placing him outside the pale of sentient life. Knowing God, man stood apart from all creation—and felt himself alone.

And yet, once experienced, this uniqueness remained inexpressible. It still does. How many adequate accounts of it survive in the history of thought? How many descriptions of it exist that really convey to us, to any human being at all, the truth that everyone, whether a great mystic or simple dolt, intuits but cannot express? Does there actually exist a man who does not know what is meant when the word "God" is uttered? Does there actually exist an animal who does? Yet when it comes to the expression of it, there is hardly a poem in the whole of literature that gives any sufficient impression. Here all is analogical, representative but not actual; everything said is "in a manner of speaking." And when by accident or grace a poet emerges who succeeds ever so slightly in giving back some impression of the reality all men experience, we honor him above every other, placing him in a category apart. All poets declare how they feel about God and count on being understood; but how many of them can give back to us our own awareness of the existence of God, make us reexperience what we all know by intuition, make apparent to us *what God is*?

Now, this "what God is," or, more properly, this "as God is," becomes the second step in Otto's analysis of the Idea of the Holy. After establishing the fundamental situation of the numinous as something manifesting itself in a general condition of creaturefeeling, he goes on to specify the object of this numinous consciousness, knowing full well, however, that only in terms of feeling can it be reflected positively in his mind. "Its nature is such that it grips or stirs the human with this and that determinative state."[19] Seeking to isolate the deepest and most fundamental element in all strongly felt religious emotion, he goes at once to that which lies outside the characteristics we usually attribute to it—such things as trust, or love, or faith unto salvation. All these things, of course, may be involved, but they do not comprise the essence of the numinous feeling. Above them and beyond them exists an element which may, quite apart from them, affect us profoundly and occupy our minds with a most bewildering strength:

Let us follow it up with every effort of sympathy and imaginative intuition wherever it is to be found, in the lives of those around us, in sudden, strong ebullitions of personal piety and the frames of mind such ebullitions evince, in the fixed and ordered solemnities of rites and liturgies, and again in the atmosphere that clings to old religious monuments and buildings—to temples and to churches.[20]

If we do so follow it, he assures us, we shall realize "that we are dealing with something for which there is only one appropriate expression, *mysterium tremendum.*" Once again, as with the specification of the numinous, he has reached back into the Latin to designate more precisely the components of what he seeks, and having done so presents us with what we intuit as the straight force of an archetype:

The feeling of it may at times come sweeping like a gentle tide, pervading the mind with a tranquil mood of deepest worship. It may pass over into a more set and lasting attribute of the soul, continuing as it were, thrillingly vibrant and resonant, until at last it dies away and the soul resumes its "profane" non-religious mood of everyday exprience. It may burst in sudden eruption up from the depths of the soul with spasms and convulsions, or lead to the strongest excitements, to intoxicated frenzy, to transport, and to ecstasy. It has its wild and demonic forms and can sink to an almost grisly horror and shuddering. It has its crude, barbaric antecedents and early manifestations, and again it may be developed into something beautiful and pure and glorious. It may become the hushed, trembling, and speechless humility of the creature in the presence of— whom or what? In the presence of that which is a *mystery* inexpressible and above all creatures.[21]

Otto is not unaware that, in calling the object of this numinous consciousness the *mysterium tremendum*, his conceptualization can only proceed negatively. As a concept, *mysterium* denotes merely what is concealed, what cannot be grasped, that which is beyond specification. But, he insists, "though what is enunciated in the word is negative, what is *meant* is something absolutely and intensely positive."[22]

This extreme disparity between positive feeling and negative concept is at the root of our inability to express the universal comprehension of "what God is." It is responsible for this astounding paradox that the most emphatic affirmation known to man can only be expressed conceptually in negative terms. But, wonder of wonders, this "pure positive" can be *experienced* in the perplexing ambivalence of our feelings, "feelings which our discussion can help make clear to us, insofar as it arouses them actually in our hearts."[23]

Before going on to a deeper analysis of what Otto means by the component elements in the numinous, it is well to state that so far as concerns Jeffers, the poet never seeks to deal with the *mysterium tremendum* as the pure "inexpressible" in the way traditional with mystical poets. That he is indeed aware of it, his work everywhere makes clear: it is the primary fact of his life; it stands before all his reflection, all his labor, all his creativity. It is for him the very charge, force, and meaning of reality. That he does not attempt to register it in its intrinsic presence is due rather to the type of religious poet he is than to any inadequacy of feeling. That is to say, as *poet* he is more the prophet than the contemplative. As such, he is concerned, once he has acknowledged its omnipresence, to adumbrate the impact of the *mysterium tremendum* upon the life of man, its social, moral, and political dimension, than to register it in its utter ineffability.

This distinction between the poet as contemplative and the poet as prophet is important, for by means of it we are able to orient the position of the artist in the broad field of religious experience. Writers on mysticism are wont to analyze it in terms of its grades, the levels of ascent from mundane reflection to infused contemplation, and they naturally see the aesthetic as an experience that one transcends as one approaches in vision the intrinsic reality of the Unapproachable. Sometimes they see art as a mere making, a virtue of the practical intellect, and hence in this way also relegate it to an inferior place in the mystical ascent. Now since many religious poets are primarily mystics—as was, for instance, St. John of the Cross—their poems do fall within this mystical context, and their voices often sound like the last murmur before the vast speechlessness possesses them, and they are indeed alone with the Alone.

However, this prevalence of the mystical element in great religious verse is deceptive. What the theoreticians fail to recognize is another kind of charismatic activity, itself directly involved with the numinous, and this, as noted above, is prophecy. Prophecy might be called the overflow of contemplation; it begins where mysticism leaves off. Whereas mysticism ascends, prophecy descends. From the psychological point of view, the contemplative experiences his abysmal inferiority to that which he approaches, and his voice dies in speechlessness. The prophet, however, experiences the divine superiority to the underextending mundane reality he confronts. It is this situation of a transcendent point of view which the *mysterium tremendum* has given him that endows the prophet with the force of authority, the almost reckless propensity for extreme declaration, and out of it the voice speaks explicitly and emphatically.

Now it is apparent that, charismatically, poetry is closer to prophecy than it is to mystical contemplation. Even in the psychological order, poetry follows inspiration rather than precedes it. Therefore it is unwise to restrict the aesthetic to its passive dimension, as an intermediary step to the divine, something to be transcended. In poetry the aesthetic becomes the *vehicle* of the divine. It is divinity plus the human tongue giving it utterance, and so crucial is its function that the tongue becomes as important as the message. Thus when it comes to specifying the grades of religious feeling, we find that Jeffers, contemplative though he be, always speaks with the authority of positive indication. He speaks as one who has experienced the *mysterium tremendum*, knows what it means, and is telling the world what he knows.

This is why when pursuing the analysis that follows throughout the course of Otto's book, we find many examples from Jeffers illustrative of these attributes, but none relating to the mystery *per se*. There is nothing of the transparent visionary condition we see in, say, the Sufi mystic: "I went from God to God, until they cried from me in me, 'O thou I.' "[24] Jeffers does not speak from the point of view of one who annuls the self as he approaches the divine—this he keeps to himself—but he does emphatically speak from the point of view of one who comes back, of divinity's specific application to the human condition, and this he shouts to the world.

However, before going on, there is a factor relevant to the *mysterium tremendum* in its infused transcendence for which Jeffers does show great concern, and that is the question of how men interpret it, the attribution made of it by those who have known it. And we may as well discuss it here before we go on to more specific effects, for by doing so we prepare ourselves to understand a good deal of what is to come in regard to the way the poet expresses himself. For every man defines himself, positively or negatively, over against the practice and the opinions of those around him.

As a religious psychologist, Jeffers is acutely aware of the impact of the *mysterium tremendum* on the individual psyche, and in his rendition of religious character among the figures of his narratives, he has depicted, at one time or another, several of the affective states we encounter in our analysis. While he himself is never in doubt about the reality of the *mysterium tremendum*, from the point of view of objective delineation, he is not uncritical. Rather, for him nothing is more revelatory of man's endemic blindness than the appalling way in which our omnivorous eccentricity misappropriates the most transcendent charismatic perception. Thus the whole of *The Women at Point Sur* is the portrayal of a man progressively destroyed by his misconception of the incredible shift in consciousness that he is undergoing, a shift entered through violation, misapplied through an obsessively fixed formula (*God thinks through action*), and jettisoned through the lust for disciples. The whole nexus of the poem is built upon the paradox of the incredible reality experienced through direct perception, progressively nullified by a malfunction of attribution.

However, setting aside for now the problem of *The Women at Point Sur*, let us consider a vignette of obvious misattribution at its crudest. Old Fraser in *Give Your Heart to the Hawks* patently simulates the *mysterium tremendum* out of emotional need and nothing else, attributing divine ordination to meteorological fact:

The rain held off; for two hundred and forty days there had been no
    rain
But one sun-drunken shower. The creek was dry rock and weary gray
    roots; the skin of the mountain crumbled
Under starved feet; the five carcasses of hawks that Lance had hung on
    the fence-wire dried without odor
In the north wind and rages of the sun.
                    Old Fraser walked under the
    moon along the farm-drive beside them,
Saying, "Lord if thou art minded to burn the whole earth

And spat off the dust from thy hands, it is well done,
The glory and the vengeance: but if anywhere
Rain falls on hills, remember I beseech thee thy servant's place,
Or the beasts die in the field." While he was praying
The moon dimmed; he felt a flutelike exultance
Flow up from the V of his ribs to his wrinkled throat:
He was not abandoned: and looked aloft and saw
A little many-colored man's-palm-size cloud
Coasting the moon from the southeast, the storm-side.
The old man exalted himself; he had power upon God; and anxiously
Repressing his joy for fear it waste the event
Beforehand, compelled his heart to remember bitterness,
His two sons lost, one dead, the other in rebellion,
And poverty and scorn and the starved cattle. "Oh Lord God,
As in old time thou didst choose one little people for thine out of all
    the earth,
So now thou hast chosen one man, one old man, foolish and poor: but
    if thy will was made up
To punish the earth, then heed not my voice but arise and punish. It is
    rank with defilement and infidelity
And the music of the evil churches." He saw a shining white form at
    the garden-gate, and for a high moment
Believed that some angel, as unto Abraham . . . It was Lance[25]

This concern regarding the attribution of the *mysterium tremen-dum*, the misconception of its nature and function by those who experience it, finds its most salient expression in a soliloquy of Jesus in the play *Dear Judas*. Written after *The Women at Point Sur*, his peak work, this play appears as a kind of afterthought and is his most unsatisfactory work. But I think this particular soliloquy is crucial because in it Jeffers most completely expresses what he regarded as Christ's misconception of the *mysterium tremendum* that had been vouchsafed him. And because Christ has been the key figure of the great epoch of man that is now closing, Jeffers purports to expose his misconception as fatal to the entire epoch, a poisonous seed staining its entire course, precipitating the fatal torque that would in the end sever it within itself and splinter it into a thousand painful fragments. Jesus speaks:

Three . . . four times in my life I have been one
    with our Father,
The night and the day, the dark seas and the little fountains, the sown
    and the desert, the morning star

And the mountains against morning and the mountain cedars, the
     sheep and the wolves, the Hebrews and the free nomads
That eat camels and worship a stone, and the sun cures them like salt
     into the marrow in the bones;
All, all, the times future and past
The hanging leaves on one tree: there is not a word nor a dream nor
     any way to declare his loveliness
Except to have felt and known, to have *been* the beauty. Even the
     cruelties and agonies that my poor Judas
Chokes on: were there in the net, shining. The hawk shone like the
     dove. Why, there it is! Exultation,
You stripped dupe? I have gathered my ruins.[26]

Thus far the *mysterium tremendum* is remembered as the inclu-
sive vision charged with wonder and the synthesis of revelation.
But now comes the attribution: out of the mouth of Jesus, the or-
thodox theological doctrine of the mystical body of Christ is in-
dicted as an unsound ego-need, a kind of lust for love as ultimate
self-congratulation:

Life after life, at the bottom of the pit comes exultation. I seem to
     remember so many nights?
In the smell of old cypresses in the garden darkness. And the means of
     power,
All clear and formed, like tangible symbols laid in my mind. Two
     thousand years are laid in my hands
Like grains of corn. Not for the power: Oh, more than power, actual
     possession. To be with my people,
In their very hearts, a part of their being, inseparable from those that
     love me, more closely touching them
Than the cloth of the inner garment touches the flesh. That this is
     tyrannous
I know, that it is love run to lust: but I will possess them. The hawk
     shines like the dove. Oh, power
Bought at the price these hands and feet and all this body perishing in
     torture will pay is holy
Their minds love terror, their souls cry to be sacrificed for: pain's
     almost the God
Of doubtful men, who tremble expecting to endure it. Their cruelty
     sublimed. And I think the brute cross itself,
Hewn down to a gibbet now, has been worshiped; it stands yet for an
     idol of life and power in the dreaming
Soul of the world and the waters under humanity, whence floating again

It will fly up heaven, and heavy with triumphant blood and renewal,
    the very nails and the beams alive.
I saw my future when I was with God; but now at length in a flashing
    moment the means: I frightfully
Lifted up drawing all men to my feet: I go a stranger passage to a
    greater dominion,
More tyrannous, more terrible, more true, than Caesar or any subduer
    of the earth before him has dared to dream of
In a dream on his bed, over the prostrate city, before the pale weary
    dawn
Creeps through his palace, through the purple fringes, between the
    polished agate pillars, to steal it away.[27]

However, though Jeffers himself rejects the attribution of
Christ as to the meaning of the *mysterium tremendum* vouchsafed
him, he does not in every instance show himself contemptuous
of it, as in the case of Old Fraser. Rather, if the attitude of the be-
liever is palpably simple and without spiritual ambition, he ac-
cords it a sympathy of treatment that is close to credence. The
Christian ingredients in the experience of Onorio Vasquez (such
as his touching plea to take the place of the crucified hawk in the
Prelude to *The Women at Point Sur*) he retains with sympathetic
expression, but the best instance is that of the Indian woman
named California in *Roan Stallion*. Abused by her drunken hus-
band on the day before Christmas, she yet is determined that her
little girl will have something for the feast, and, late as Johnny's
callousness in bed has detained her, she hitches the mare Dora to
the buckboard and drives to Monterey. Coming back in the dark,
she runs into trouble at the ford. Try as she might, she cannot
make her horse go through:

              The mare
Stopped, her two forefeet in the water. She touched with the whip.
    The mare plodded ahead and halted.
Then California thought of prayer: "Dear little Jesus,
Dear baby Jesus born to-night, your head was shining
Like silver candles. I've got a baby too, only a girl. You had light
    wherever you walked.
Dear baby Jesus give me light." Light streamed: rose, gold, rich
    purple, hiding the ford like a curtain.
The gentle thunder of water was a noise of wing-feathers, the fans of
    paradise lifting softly.

The child afloat on radiance had a baby face, but the angels had birds'
heads, hawks' heads,
Bending over the baby, weaving a web of wings about him. He held in
the small fat hand
A little snake with golden eyes, and California could see clearly on the
under radiance
The mare's pricked ears, a sharp black fork against the shining
light-fall. But it dropped; the light of heaven
Frightened poor Dora. She backed; swung up the water,
And nearly oversetting the buggy turned and scrambled backward; the
iron wheel-tires rang on boulders.[28]

Jeffers accepts this incident as something ostensibly true and
makes no attempt to undermine its veracity, as he does in *Dear Ju-
das*, when the miracles of Christ are presented as trumped-up in-
stances in a case of programmatically contrived spiritual ambition.

As a final example, the poem "A Redeemer" might be in-
stanced, for the Christian element is here, and denigrated, but
the attribution is otherwise. Here the man has obviously experi-
enced the *mysterium tremendum*, and he responds to it in an ex-
treme way, taking upon himself a kind of Christ-appropriation.
But the values he expresses, as attribution, are Jeffers's own. The
poet would seem, by this device, to risk jeopardizing his philos-
ophy by putting it in the mouth of a person of questionable men-
tality, but he obviously does not fear this, moving through the
thread of discourse without undue self-consciousness—in fact,
with complete ease. This ease of handling, whether treating the
miracle of the ford in *Roan Stallion* or the placing of his own values
in the mouth of a questionable mind, shows, I believe, the pri-
macy of Jeffers as dramatic artist to any of the philosophical tenets
he holds so passionately. Give him a dramatic situation, and he
treats it with authority, no matter how much he seems to have
jeopardized it with philosophical tendentiousness:

The road had steepened and the sun sharpened on the high ridges; the
stream probably was dry,
Certainly not to be come to down the pit of the canyon. We stopped
for water at the one farm
In all that mountain. The trough was cracked with drought, the moss
on the boards dead, but an old dog
Rose like a wooden toy at the house-door silently. I said "There will be
water somewhere about,"

And when I knocked a man showed us a spring of water. Though his
    hair was nearly white I judged him
Forty years old at most. His eyes and voice were muted. It is likely he
    kept his hands hidden,
I failed to see them until we had dipped the spring. He stood then on
    the lip of the great slope
And looked westward over an incredible country to the far hills that
    dammed the sea-fog: it billowed
Above them, cascaded over them, it never crossed them, gray standing
    flood. He stood gazing, his hands
Were clasped behind him; I caught a glimpse of serous red under the
    fingers, and looking sharply
When they drew apart saw that both hands were wounded. I said
    "Your hands are hurt." He twitched them from sight,
But after a moment having earnestly eyed me displayed them. The
    wounds were in the hearts of the palms,
Pierced to the backs like stigmata of crucifixion. The horrible raw flesh
    protruded, glistening
And granular, not scabbed, nor a sign of infection. "These are old
    wounds." He answered, "Yes, they don't heal." He stood
Moving his lips in silence, his back against that fabulous basin of
    mountains, fold beyond fold,
Patches of forest and scarps of rock, high domes of dead gray pasture
    and gray beds of dry rivers,
Clear and particular in the burning air, too bright to appear real, to the
    last range
The fog from the ocean like a stretched compacted thunderstorm
    overhung; and he said gravely:
"I pick them open. I made them long ago with a clean steel. It is only a
    little to pay—"
He stretched and flexed the fingers, I saw his sunburnt lips whiten in a
    line compressed together,
"If only it proves enough for a time—to save so many." I searched his
    face for madness but that
Is often invisible, a subtle spirit. "There never," he said, "was any
    people earned so much ruin.
I love them, I am trying to suffer for them. It would be bad if I should
    die, I am careful
Against excess." "You think of the wounds," I said, "of Jesus?" He
    laughed angrily and frowned, stroking
The fingers of one hand with the other. "Religion is the people's
    opium. Your little Jew-God?
My pain," he said with pride, "is voluntary.

They have done what never was done before. Not as a people takes a
    land to love it and be fed,
A little, according to need and love, and again a little; sparing the
    country tribes, mixing
Their blood with theirs, their minds with all the rocks and rivers, their
    flesh with the soil: no, without hunger
Wasting the world and your own labor, without love possessing, not
    even your hands to the dirt but plows
Like blades of knives; heartless machines; houses of steel: using and
    despising the patient earth . . .
Oh, as a rich man eats a forest for profit and a field for vanity, so you
    came west and raped
The continent and brushed its people to death. Without need, the
    weak skirmishing hunters, and without mercy.
Well, God's a scarecrow; no vengeance out of old rags. But there are
    acts breeding their own reversals
In their own bellies from the first day. I am here" he said—and broke
    off suddenly and said "They take horses
And give them sicknesses through hollow needles, their blood saves
    babies: I am here on the mountain making
Antitoxin for all the happy towns and farms, the lovely blameless
    children, the terrible
Arrogant cities. I used to think them terrible: their gray prosperity,
    their pride: from up here
Specks of mildew.

        But when I am dead and all you with whole hands
        think of nothing but happiness,
Will you go mad and kill each other? Or horror come over the ocean on
    wings and cover your sun?
I wish," he said trembling, "I had never been born."

His wife came from the door while he was talking. Mine asked her
    quietly, "Do you live all alone here,
Are you not afraid?" "Certainly not," she answered, "he is always
    gentle and loving. I have no complaint
Except his groans in the night keep me awake often. But when I think
    of other women's
Troubles: my own daughter's: I'm older than my husband, I have been
    married before: deep is my peace."[29]

But when the question arises as to the *correct* attribution of the
power experienced in the *mysterium tremendum*, Jeffers, in a thou-
sand instances studded throughout his verse, declares that attri-

bution must be foregone, that the experience is its own reward, that for the truly self-possessed to be God-possessed ought to suffice, that the fundamental error lies in the temptation to help others through the attribution of its energies. In his "Meditation on Saviors," written at the same time as "A Redeemer" and appearing in the same volume, he examines the problem with great closeness—and incidentally achieves one of his best examples of expository verse. Attribution, he declares, is the temptation of the would-be savior rather than an authentic solution, because death is, actually, its own deliverer:

> a huge gift reserved quite overwhelms them at the end;
> they are able then to be still and not cry.

And having touched a little of the beauty and seen a little of the beauty of things, magically grow
Across the funeral fire or the hidden stench of burial themselves into the beauty they admired,
Themselves into the God, themselves into the sacred steep unconsciousness
. . .
        they need no savior,
salvation comes and takes them by force,
It gathers them into the great kingdom of dust and stone, the blown storms, the stream's-end ocean.[30]

And he concludes with the only acknowledgment as to the value of consciousness he ever concedes:

With this advantage over their granite grave-marks, of having realized the petulant human consciousness
Before, and then the greatness, the peace: drunk from both pitchers[31]

And finishes with his only concession to the powers of love, but sheerly qualified by the necessity of turning love from itself to its absolute, and so be freed of its obsessiveness:

But while he lives let each man make his health in his mind, to love the coast opposite humanity,
And so be freed of love, laying it like bread on the water, it is worst turned inward, it is best shot farthest.
Love, the mad wine of good and evil, the saint's and murderer's, the mote in the eye that makes its object

Shine the sun black; the trap in which it is better to catch the inhuman
   God than the hunter's own image.[32]

There seems to be an implicit acknowledgment here that love
is the aftereffect, not the consequence, of the *mysterium tremen-
dum*. The central problem of life remains the problem of attribu-
tion: what one does with one's power, to whom or upon what
does one lavish one's love? But mostly Jeffers fears love as the trap
that sucks the savior to its service. By qualifying its imperatives,
he hopes to place himself in a relationship which will free him to
consummate its inception without succumbing to its force.

III. DEMONIC DREAD

During World War II there was a popular saying to the effect
that "There are no atheists in the foxholes." It served well as a
religious slogan for the general public when so many lives were
in jeopardy, but it never convinced any atheists, at least none I
knew. My best friends, or those who happened to be safely out
of the foxholes, disgustedly demurred: "Put a man under insu-
perable strain for days and weeks, threaten his rationality
through a crescendo of terrific assaults on his sensibility, reduce
him to a quivering jelly of benumbed consciousness, drive him
back upon the most elemental, the most unreflective neural re-
actions, afflict him until the very substratum of his being is in-
duced to clamor out a name implanted in his infancy—'God!'—
and then gloat triumphantly, 'There are no atheists in the fox-
holes!' This is detestable. It is religion's last ditch resort to a for-
mula more pathetic than the unfortunate victim in the foxholes.
But as for a thinking man's solution to the problem of God, it is
absurd."

Neither Christian nor atheist at that time, this disclaimer never
really convinced me. I had experienced religious awe enough
times not to require foxhole experience to verify my sense of the
absolute. I knew that awe is the product of vulnerability, and to
the reflective man it does not take conditions of extremity to bring
home to him how vulnerable he actually is. We do not experience
the change in attitude from agnosticism to religious belief by vir-
tue of rational reflection. Rather, we are brought to our knees by

an experience of such profundity, of such import, of such awe, that we are unable any longer to sustain detachment. Awe seizes us like a fist, asserts itself into the field of our emotional comprehension, and renders us incapable of defiance. Like atheists who lose their objectivity in the foxhole, we learn the cry of the heart that brooks no denial, and never, when it at last occurs, begrudge the extremities that life had to exact of us by way of our assaulted sensibility in order to render us palpable to everything that this awe now offers. If we are confronted instantly with the problem of attribution, neither do we begrudge all the soul-searching it will exact of us, for the decision we arrive at will be by virtue of the peace it yields us. Our wrestling has just begun, but at least it has begun.

For though attribution (as we saw in the last chapter) may be the central problem of life (how we employ the surging energies released by our experience of the divine, the *mysterium tremendum*), before the problem of its use can be solved, it is necessary to know what it is. Only those who have experienced it have been tempted by it. Only those who have tasted power have craved to employ power. Existing before love, that "mad wine of good and evil, the saint's and murderer's," awe itself awaits as the primary experience that preestablishes action and constitutes the datum out of which all salvific attempts, be they good or bad, will pour. Jeffers may be a prophet by virtue of his attempt to rectify the course of human action, but he is intensely preprophetic in his power to understand, to grasp the shuddering immediacy of the superior reality that constitutes the essence of the religious experience.

It is for this reason that, when Otto begins to analyze the elements of the *mysterium tremendum* itself, we feel we are in a position to move up with Jeffers beyond detached objectification to experience his own direct involvement. The first of these is what Otto calls "the Element of Awefulness" and which he finds designated not so much by concepts as by what he calls "ideograms," in this case the ideogram of "absolute unapproachability."[33] Having observed, as we saw, that conceptually *mysterium* denotes what is hidden and esoteric, what is beyond conception or understanding, and that the term does *not* define the object more positively in its qualitative character, a matter to be experienced only in our feelings, so too, he goes on to say, with the *tremendum*, where *tremor* is in itself merely the perfectly familiar and "natural" emotion of *fear*. Here, also, the term is taken, aptly enough but still only by analogy, to denote a quite specific kind of emotional response, a response wholly distinct from the feeling of being afraid, and it goes back to the most primitive roots of religion. "Let us give a little further consideration to the first crude, primitive forms in which this 'numinous dread' or *awe* shows itself. It is the mark which really characterizes the so-called 'religion of primitive man,' and there it appears as 'demonic dread.'"[34] We begin, therefore, this probe into the complex field of the element of awefulness by a search to establish the presence of demonic dread in the work of Jeffers.

It is Otto's contention that this absolutely basic and seemingly atavistic emotion constitutes the fundamental element in religious experience—and that however much a higher development seems to supersede and outstrip it, something of its underlying intensity must be, and in fact is, retained:

This crudely naive and primordial emotional disturbance, and the fantastic images to which it gives rise, are later overborn and ousted by more highly developed forms of the numinous emotion, with all its mysterious impelling power. But even when this has long attained its higher and purer mode of expression it is possible for the primitive types of excitation that were formerly a part of it to break out in the soul in all their original naivete and so to be experienced afresh.[35]

Jeffers is well aware of this "crudely naive and primordial emotional disturbance" and often depicts those fantastic images to which it gives rise. His narratives are rich with incidents of the preternatural, manifestations of the occult, and strange epiphanies. That such manifestations of the preternatural are truly relevant, constituting authentic adjuncts of religious experience, Otto makes clear and is especially concerned to dissociate them from any kind of assimilation to a purely natural fear:

That this is so is shown by the potent attraction again and again exercised by the element of horror and "shudder" in ghost stories, even among persons of high all-around education. It is a remarkable fact that the physical reaction to which this unique "dread" of the uncanny gives rise is also unique, and is not found in the case of any "natural" fear or terror.

We say "my blood ran icy cold," and "my flesh crept." The "cold blood" feeling may be a symptom of ordinary, natural fear, but there is something non-natural or supernatural about the symptom of "creeping flesh."[36]

Otto is careful, too, to skirt the natural tendency to assume this shudder is a matter of simple intensity, fear compounded by fear until it touches a degree that threatens the ego:

And any one who is capable of more precise introspection must recognize that the distinction between such a "dread" and natural fear is not simply one of degree and intensity. The awe or "dread" *may* indeed be so overwhelmingly great that it seems to penetrate to the very marrow, making the man's hair bristle and his limbs quake. But it may also steal upon him almost unobserved as the gentlest of agitations, a mere fleeting shadow passing across his mood. It has therefore nothing to do with intensity, and no natural fear passes over into it merely by being intensified. I may be beyond all measure afraid and terrified without there being even a trace of the feeling of uncanniness in my emotion.[37]

Considered under such a light, most of the difficulties which Carpenter wrestles with, for instance, in his chapter on "Philosophy and Religion," wherein the inconsistencies of Jeffers's attitude to supernaturalism are noted, fall into perspective. "How can he justify," Carpenter asks, "the use of supernatural beings in his own poetry, when he attacks the supernatural pretensions of orthodox religions?"[38]

Actually, what Jeffers attacks in orthodoxy is, as we saw, the *attribution* made of the presence of supernatural phenomena, not the existence of such phenomena, which of course he freely employs. Of these instances, the short poem "Local Legend" from the *Hungerfield* volume will serve.

Two Spanish cowhands from Monterey
Riding, a moonless midnight, to their beds on the coast
Heard a child crying in the pinewood
On the ridge of the Carmel hill; they beat the bushes and found
A naked babe laid on the needle-floor
In the dark screaming. They picked it up, how could they leave it
    there?
One of them huddled it under his coat;
They had not ridden a hundred yards when a fountain of fire
Spouted from the babe's mouth: the man

Shrieked, and flung his foundling into the bushes; they never stopped
    galloping
Until they'd forded the Carmel River
And let the blown horses breathe.—That is all. The story,
Senseless as other supernaturalisms,
Might even be true, for who would take the trouble to invent it?
But most of us, one time or another,
Have taken unhappy causes or hopes to heart, and gotten well burnt. [39]

Other instances that might be mentioned are the Christ-child vi-
sion in *Roan Stallion*, the shore-line ghosts and other preternat-
ural powers in *Tamar*, the calling up of his father's ghost in
"Come, Little Birds," and the talking stones in *The Tower Beyond
Tragedy*. Rather than attempting to localize these examples in
terms of Jeffers's philosophy, we can see their place in his work
more consistently when we regard them as instances of the close-
ness of his religious feeling to its primordial sources, authentic
elements of universal religious experience.

Thus in "Mara," when the man Ferguson encounters the per-
sonification of his split mind and engages it in dialogue, most
contemporary poets would be content to let the incident stand as
a purely psychic encounter; but Jeffers, with his telling and in-
stinctive naiveté, suddenly concretizes the episode into the cat-
egory of "demonic dread" by sending the man's dog, hackles
raised, out of his presence. "Mara," written at a time of great wea-
riness for the poet, is not a great poem, but at several points in it
Jeffers reveals his instantaneous capacity to go the limit, letting us
understand his radical closeness to the primitive religious spirit.

But this astonishing accessibility to movements of primordial
feeling is perhaps most powerfully demonstrated in the narrative
poem *Hungerfield*, when the protagonist fights Death in physical
combat. In this last of his narratives, the poet is obviously weary
of life, terribly longing for finality, and patently disinclined to
maintain the maximum psychic intensity that pervades his best
narratives. But suddenly in Hungerfield's encounter with Death,
something in the poet, despite his weariness, lets go. One feels
he is speaking directly out of himself, out of his own unconscious
heart, when he says of the man that "While his mind lied his
blood and body believed." The generalized narrative mentality is
secular and sophisticated, but the feeling-sources of demonic
dread are as primitive as Beowulf. Listen to the long development

of mood that readies all for the moment of decisiveness. Hungerfield's mother Alcmena is failing, and Hungerfield tells her she will not die:

> It is a common lie to the dying, and I too have told it; but
> Hungerfield—
> While his mind lied his blood and body believed. He had seen Death
> and he would see him again.
> He was waiting for his enemy.
> Night deepened around the house; the
> sea-waves came up into the stream,
> And the stream fought them; the cliffs and standing rocks black and
> bone-still
> Stood in the dark. There were no stars, there were some little sparkles
> of glowworms on the wet ground,
> If you looked closely, and shapes of things, and the shifting foam-line.
> The vast phantasmagoria of night
> Proceeded around that central throat begging for breath, and
> Hungerfield
> Sat beside it, rigid and motionless as the rocks but his fingers
> twitching, hunched like a cat
> To spring and tear.[40]

Thus the scene is delineated, suspenseful, bated, a mood of contained consequence, of impending urgency:

> Then the throat clicked and ceased. Hungerfield looked
> at it; when he looked back
> The monster was in the room. It was a column of heavy darkness in
> the dim lamplight, but the arrogant head
> Was clear to see. That damned sneer on his face. Hungerfield felt his
> hair rise like a dog's
> And heard Death say scornfully: "Quiet yourself, poor man, make no
> disturbance; it is not for you.
> I have come for the old woman Alcmena Hungerfield, to whom death
> Will be more kind than life." Hungerfield saw his throat and sprang at
> it. But he was like a man swimming
> A lake of corpses, the newly harvested souls from all earth's fields,
> faint shrieks and whispers, Death's company.
> He smote their dim heads with his hands and their bowels with his feet
> And swam on them. He reached Death's monstrous flesh and they
> cleared away. It had looked like a shadow,
> It was harder than iron. The throat was missed, they stood and
> hugged each other like lovers; Hungerfield

Drove his knee to the groin. Death laughed and said,
"I am not a man," and the awful embrace tightened
On the man's loins; he began to be bent backward, writhing and
    sobbing; he felt the years of his age
Bite at his heart like rats: he was not yet fifty: but it is known that little
    by little God abandons men
When thirty's past. Experience and cunning may perhaps increase
But power departs. He struck short at the throat and was bent further
    backward, and suddenly
Flung himself back and fell, dragging Death down with him, twisting
    in the fall, and weasel-quick on the floor
Tore at the throat: then the horrible stench and hopelessness of dead
    bodies filled the dim air; he thought
He had wounded Death. What? The iron force and frame of nature
    with his naked hands? It bubbled and gasped,
"You fool—what have you done!" The iron flesh in his grip melted like
    a summer corpse, and turning liquid
Slid from his hands. He stood up foaming and groped for it; there was
    nothing. He saw in the stair-door Arab, and Ross his brother, and
    the hired cattlehand
Staring with eyes like moons. They had heard a chair crash and seen
    the fury; Arab had screamed like a hawk,
But no one heard her; now she stood moaning, gazing at him. But
    Ross entered the room and walked
Carefully wide around him to their mother's bed. The old woman was
    sitting up and breathed easily, saying
"I saw it all. Listen: they are taking him away." A strain of mournful
    music was heard, from the house
Flitting up the black night. This was the time—it was near midnight
    here—for a quarter of an hour
Nobody died. Disease went on, and the little peripheral prophetic
    wars, the famines and betrayals,
Neither man nor beast died, though they might cry for him. Death,
    whom we hate and love, had met a worse monster
And could not come.[41]

The almost unbelievable poetic audacity of a writer who can as-
sume the risks of such narration is only to be accounted for by
reference to the concept of authority—a poet's incalculable sense
of the authority of his craft and his vocation.

    We have shown Jeffers's proclivity for demonic dread in the full
potential of its uncanny and terrifying horror, but Otto has noted
that it may also steal upon a man almost unobserved, arising as

the gentlest of agitations, a mere fleeting shape passing across his mood. Jeffers too knows this. In "Haunted Country," written during the period of his choicest lyrics, the poem touches such an element in a beautifully modulated aesthetic experience. Demonic dread flickers like foxfire in and about the evocative imagery, the morose concepts, fitfully illuminating the specifications of detail:

Here the human past is dim and feeble and alien to us
Our ghosts draw from the crowded future,
Fixed as the past how could it fail to drop weird shadows
And make strange murmurs about twilight?
In the dawn twilight metal falcons flew over the mountain,
Multitudes, and faded in the air; at moonrise
The farmer's girl by the still river is afraid of phantoms,
Hearing the pulse of a great city
Move on the water-meadow and stream off south; the country's
Children for all their innocent minds
Hide dry and bitter lights in the eye, they dream without knowing it
The inhuman years to be accomplished,
The inhuman powers, the servile cunning under pressure,
In a land grown old, heavy and crowded.
There are happy places that fate skips; here is not one of them;
The tides of the brute womb, the excess
And weight of life spilled out like water, the last migration
Gathering against this holier valley-mouth
That knows its fate beforehand, the flow of the womb, banked back
By the older flood of the ocean, to swallow it.[42]

Excess is the prolonged and abiding fault of Robinson Jeffers, in art if not in life, but how beautiful are the forms with which he endows it, and how close his excesses cleave to that cosmic Excess before which the soul of man must cower. In its grip, demonic dread becomes for him a kind of appetite by which he savors the divine.

Jeffers, then, is well aware not only of the dread but its transmutation into higher forms of awareness. In this he accommodates himself within the main current of religious consciousness, and no one among comtemporary religious writers more fittingly illustrates a certain retention, the value of which Otto insists upon, in the appropriation of primitive within sophisticated religious states:

Though the numinous emotion in its completest development shows a world of difference from the mere "demonic dread," yet not even at the highest level does it belie its pedigree of kindred. Even when the worship of the "demons" has long since reached the higher level of worship of "gods," these gods still retain as *numina* something of the "ghost" in the impress they make on the feelings of the worshipper, viz., the peculiar quality of the uncanny, and "aweful" which survives with the quality of exaltedness and sublimity or is symbolized by means of it. And this softened though it is, does not disappear even on the highest level of all, where the worship of God is at its purest. Its disappearance would be indeed an essential loss. The "shudder" reappears in a form ennobled beyond measure where the soul, held speechless, trembles inwardly to the farthest fibre of its being.[43]

"O passionately at peace," cries Jeffers, speaking of Night in his magnificent poem of that name, "you being secure will pardon / The blasphemies of glowworms, the lamp in my tower, the fretfulness / Of cities, the cressets of the planets, the pride of the stars."[44] And he goes on to scale out the dimension that dwarfs the mind into its underrealms of instinctive awe:

This August night in a rift of cloud Antares reddens,
The great one, the ancient torch, a lord among lost children,
The earth's orbit doubled would not girdle his greatness, one fire
Globed, out of grasp of the mind enormous; but to you, O Night
What? Not a spark? What flicker of a spark in the faint far glimmer
Of a lost fire dying in the desert, dim coals of a sand-spit the Bedouins
Wandered from at dawn . . . Ah singing prayer to what gulfs tempted
Suddenly are you more lost? To us the near-hand mountain
Be a measure of height, the tide-worn cliff at the sea-gate a measure of
    continuance.[45]

Or suddenly he can take the veritable shudder itself and affirm it directly, as it comes into him, registering it with the shock of direct impact, powerful and intense, yet partaking of the heights rather than the crudity of the experience:

I am past childhood, I look at this ocean and the fishing birds, the
    streaming skerries, the shining water,
The foam-heads, the exultant dawn-light going west, the pelicans,
    their huge wings half folded, plunging like stones.

Whatever it is catches my heart in its hands, whatever it is makes me
    shudder with love

And painful joy and the tears prickle . . . the Greeks were not its
    inventors[46]

No better instance can be found of the combination of creature-
feeling and its quality of the soul submerged in a power greater
than itself, together with that other feeling of absolute unap-
proachability and its accent of almost revulsion from and terror
before a majesty greater than one is worthy to contemplate, than
the episode in *Roan Stallion* when the woman California breaks
free and rides to the hill summit to immolate herself before the
vastness of the world below and the numinous power localized
in the presence of the stallion.

                    She stood then,
Shaking. Enormous films of moonlight
Trailed down from the height. Space, anxious whiteness, vastness.
    Distant beyond conception the shining ocean
Lay light like a haze along the ledge and doubtful world's end. Little
    vapors gleaming, and little
Darknesses on the far chart underfoot symbolized wood and valley;
    but the air was the element, the moon-
Saturate arcs and spires of the air.
                         Here is solitude, here on the calvary,
    nothing conscious
But the possible God and the cropped grass, no witness, no eye but
    that misformed one, the moon's past fullness.
Two figures on the shining hill, woman and stallion, she kneeling to
    him, brokenly adoring.
He cropping the grass, shifting his hooves, or lifting the long head to
    gaze over the world,
Tranquil and powerful. She prayed aloud, "O God, I am not good
    enough, O fear, O strength, I am draggled.
Johnny and other men have had me, and O clean power! Here am I,"
    she said, falling before him,
And crawled to his hooves.[47]

Quite enough has been instanced to establish the centrality to
Jeffers's power of this underlying attitude. If he has been called
overwhelming, it is because his heart is founded on an awareness
of power that outreaches any dimension of the mind, is actually
the source of reality itself, the power that, in keeping all in being,
sustains the poet in his incorrigibly innocent heart.

✦

TWO

✦

The Wine Cup of This Fury

✦

For thus saith the Lord God of Israel unto me;
Take the wine cup of this fury at my hand,
And cause all the nations, to whom I shall send thee,
To drink it. And they shall drink, and be moved,
And be mad, because of the sword
That I will send among them.

Jeremiah 25: 15–16

✦

I. THE TORCHES OF VIOLENCE

In the mid-1920's, when the presence of Robinson Jeffers burst so emphatically upon the fervid American literary consciousness, the country at large was awash in a tide of prosperity that exceeded anything in its history. It was an excess which, since so little military expenditure existed to absorb it, poured directly into luxuries and investment spending. Frederick Lewis Allen gives a sketch of the frantic times in his book *Only Yesterday*. There we learn that a sizeable portion of the surplus wealth was siphoned into the real estate extravaganza known as the Florida boom, which calls to mind a familiar tenet: that the force of Jeffers's initial impact was determined largely by social excesses current at the time, aberrations which his point of view was calculated to rebuke.

Radcliffe Squires writes: "While the praise of these first admirers was wild, its intensity is perhaps to be comprehended as religious. In an era of bathtub gin, spangled flappers, and economic frivolity, Jeffers's attack on man was chastening."[1] With so many literate expatriates disowning American commercialism for European culture, the general Jeffersean indictment could be enthusiastically applauded. And if readers could actually welcome such extreme castigation, accept it as salutary, and give praise to its prophet, writers have not hesitated to credit the times rather than the naked power of the verse itself.

And certain coincidences do favor this conjecture. The poet was just composing *The Women at Point Sur*, the prelude to which features a titanic Pacific storm moving in from the sea to devastate the excrescence of civilization like a judgment of God out of the Old Testament. Even as he wrote, the situation in Florida was verifying his intuition, giving it a somber prophetic relevance. Allen would recall that "two hurricanes showed what a Soothing Tropic Breeze could do when it got a running start from the West Indies"; and as he spells out the consequences, his prose becomes almost lyrical:

No malevolent Providence bent upon the teaching of humility could have struck with a more precise aim than the second and worst of these Florida hurricanes. It concentrated upon the exact region where the boom had been noisiest and most hysterical—the region about Miami. Hitting the Gold Coast early in the morning of September 18, 1926, it piled the waters of Biscayne Bay into the lovely Venetian developments, deposited a five-masted steel schooner high in the street at Coral Gables, tossed big steam yachts upon the avenues of Miami, picked up trees, lumber, pipes, tiles, debris, and even small automobiles and sent them crashing into houses, ripped the roofs off thousands of jerry-built cottages and villas, almost wiped out the town of Moor Haven on Lake Okeechobee, and left behind it some four hundred dead, sixty-three hundred injured, and fifty thousand homeless.[2]

Reading *Point Sur* today, we have forgotten the pertinence of its appearance, but its first readers, picking it up in the bookshops the following spring with that disaster fresh in their minds, could only have surmised that this author took his text from recent history.

The image of Jeffers as implacable judge, rebuker, and chastiser of erring mankind was therefore powerfully established, but much as it seemed an advantage at the time (if notoriety is ever an advantage), events were soon to prove otherwise. Over and over history teaches it, never letting the prophet forget that his celebrated predictive dooms, so ingratiatingly welcomed from the pit of corruption, redound viciously against him when the blow has fallen and the culprit bleeds. "If Jeffers' poetry in the 1920s castigated a society whose feeling of guilt demanded the castigation," Squires notes, "the whip seemed excessive when an economic depression descended. People felt they were sufficiently chastened by the collapse of the stock market."[3] Doubtless they were. But what they had to learn was that Jeffers was not indicting the transient excesses of an inflationary bubble. It would take more than an economic depression to appease *this* spirit.

Yet if Jeffers's fall from grace can be attributed to aloofness, and indifference to any change of heart in his readers, should it not be accounted to his credit that he declined to temporize, refused to truckle to mere popularity? On the contrary, this kind of integrity lays one open to a very grave aesthetic charge: the failure to develop. "How much of the appeal of Yeats, for example," wrote a commentator at Jeffers's death, "or O'Neill, or Thomas Mann, to speak only of modern artists, would be lost without the satisfying movement from Early to Middle to Late?"[4] Actually, the three periods can be discerned easily enough in Jeffers, but the difference is not of the kind that ingratiates, and the charge may as well be acknowledged: his life simply does not witness to that kind of aesthetic fluency.

And it is, after all, a criterion more appealing to one's contemporaries than to posterity, which looks back rather favorably on the massive, monolithic figure. Safely dead, the great intransigents console men for the precarious state of their own existence, the disquieting impermanence of their passionate concerns. The charge recurs frequently in the lifetimes of large, obsessive, charismatic figures. Whitman endured it. Hardy and Ibsen had to face it. Wagner and Nietzsche—each was accused of it. In the related field of religion the same structure is heard. "Oh, no! Here he comes again," groaned the courtiers and chancery attendants of pre-exilic Jerusalem as Jeremiah unrolled another scroll. "Doom! doom! doom! Has he *never* anything constructive to say?" As a matter of fact he has, but given the intentness of their own heavily indicted preoccupations, they seem unable to hear it. And so it is with Jeffers. Cut to the cast of the great nay-sayers, he must face the charge:

The deficiencies, the idiosyncrasies, even the original, very personal strengths that one could accept in the early poems became tedious, empty and unconvincing when repeated for the hundredth time. One begins, probably unfairly, to suspect the poet's own sincerity.

The same spasmodic-Gothic graveyard imagery, the buckets of blood, the ever-lasting hawk-symbols and rock-symbols and bone-symbols; the inability to evoke any but a small family of mad Jeffersean characters, all incestuous or murderous or parent-hating, all violently rhapsodic, all death-wishing; the tasteless supernaturalism, the adolescent perversions of Christianity, the attempts to translate a misunderstood modern science into modern poetry; above all, the insistent "inhumanism." . . . Even the most sympathetic critics were disappointed as book after book came out, and no new paths were taken, no change, no self-renewal occurred.

Mark Van Doren, who all but "discovered" Jeffers' first major book, already saw, while still affording high praise to his second, the dangers of his *idée fixe*: "He seems to be knocking his head to pieces against the night."[5]

And so, doubtless, in the immemorial way of the prophet, he was. Since it was a religious, not a literary, solution, Jeffers went right on with the head-knocking. After all, it was the night he was knocking against, and the night does not change. Neither does man, and since he does not, the need never stops.

And still today, if he remains famous for anything, it is for his immense retributive castigation. Nor can it be denied that through the whole body of his mature work, the fierce point of affliction is never mitigated: storms lash, lightnings flicker, waves surge, thunders crash, earthquakes shudder. Mankind flinches under a host of vindictive sentences: bones are broken, bodies are smashed, eyes gouged out, pain fletches its lividness upon the bodies of defenseless victims. God is wrath, nothing but wrath. The only solace is the solace of expiation; the only peace the peace of purgation.

Or so it seems. Jeffers conceives, ultimately, of this expiation and this purgation as something absolutely total—"For man will be blotted out, the blithe earth die, the brave sun / Die blind and blacken to the heart."[6] The anguishes of the many victims are strictly intermediary. Nothing will do until the final consummation, until the serene, intense cosmos is delivered of man's presence. Thus in *The Tower Beyond Tragedy* Jeffers's redaction of Aeschylus, Cassandra, the violated prophetess, predicts the apotheosis of human inventiveness in the submarine and the airplane and the wireless, envisions beyond them the encroachment of universal frost, an extension of the polar icecaps over the whole globe, enveloping the world like a white cloth. In the mouth of his prophetess, Jeffers makes it clear that this is retribution, and that it is divine:

> An end shall be surely,
> Though unnatural things are accomplished, they breathe in the sea's
>   depth,
> They swim in the air, they bridle the cloud-leaper lightning to carry
>   their messages:
> Though the eagles of the east and the west and the falcons of the north
>   were not quieted, you have seen a white cloth

Cover the lands from the north and the eyes of the lands and the claws
    of the hunters,
The mouths of the hungry with snow
Were filled, and their claws
Took hold upon ice in the pasture, a morsel of ice was their catch in the
    rivers,
That pure white quietness
Waits on the heads of the mountains, not sleep but death, will the fire
Of burnt cities and ships in that year warm you my enemies? The
    frost, the old frost,
Like a cat with a broken-winged bird it will play with you,
It will nip and let go; you will say it is gone, but the next
Season it increases: O clean, clean
White and most clean, colorless quietness,
Without trace, without trail, without stain in the garment, drawn
    down
From the poles to the girdle. . . . I have known one Godhead
To my sore hurt: I am growing to come to another: O grave and kindly
Last of the lords of the earth, I pray you lead my substance
Speedily into another shape, make me grass, Death, make me stone,
Make me air to wander free between the stars and the peaks; but cut
    humanity
Out of my being, that is the wound that festers in me.[7]

The dramatic situation is Greek, but the language is that of the
King James Bible, sufficient testimony to the divine attribution in
the prophetic voice. Change his tune to appease a chorus of
protesters? Twenty years later, in another war, he recalled his pro-
phetess, and addressed a poem to her:

Therefore the poets honey their truth with lying; but religion-
Venders and political men
Pour from the barrel, new lies on the old, and are praised for kindly
Wisdom. Poor bitch, be wise.
No: you'll still mumble in a corner a crust of truth, to men
And gods disgusting.—You and I, Cassandra.[8]

    In the overall view of Jeffersean writing, however, the retribu-
tion motif is not so much spelled out as received, assumed within
an omnipresent castigational atmosphere informing poem after
poem, suffusing passage after passage of the long narratives. It
becomes the climate in which most of the action and much of the

speculation take place, determining in intensity what happens as
well as being determined by it. Thus, the opening of *Solstice* em-
ploys both inference and explication:

Under this rain-wind the sombre magnificence of the coast
Remembers virtues older than Christ; I see the blood-brown wound of
     the river in the black bay,
The shark-tooth waves, the white gulls beaten on the black cloud, the
     streaming black rocks. Ah be strong, storm.
Pride and ferocity are virtues as well as love. I call to mind the dark
     mountains along the south,
The rock-heads in the cloud and the roaring cliffs, the redwoods
     cracking under the weight of wind,
These changes wash clean the mind.
We even can face our lives, to bear them or change them. I call to mind
Against our meanness, the bitter crawling meanness of human lives—
     not to damn all—[9]

What he calls to mind, given the backdrop against which he has
chosen to establish it, is going to have to be larger than life, as
fierce as the elements, more pain-wracked and tormented and re-
lentless than the powers that work upon it. In the general afflic-
tive atmosphere, it must suffer existence as the penitent suffers
the lash: the subsistent condition of life.

Nevertheless, though this immense castigational atmosphere
is everywhere, is virtually omnipresent, what emerges upon ex-
amination is something absolutely impersonal and abstract. Jef-
fers's God is not moral. Man may be punished, but it is not for his
sins. Retribution is rarely occasioned by the immorality of specific
social acts. The good are maimed with the evil, the innocent die
with the guilty. No, what is being indicted is consciousness itself.
In *The Women at Point Sur*, the mad minister Barclay's break with
ethical Christianity devolves directly from this recognition that
God is transmoral:

     The God of the stars has taken his hand out of the laws and
        has dropped them empty
As you draw your hand out of a glove. When I saw that he had
     withdrawn himself out of the churches
I left the church, I was a minister, I told them
God is not here.

. . .

> "God thinks through action, I have watched him,
> through the acts of men fighting and the acts of women
> As much as through the immense courses of the stars; all the acts, all
> the bodies; who dares to enclose him
> With *this is right* and *that's wrong*, shut his thought with scruples, blind
> him against discoveries, blind his eyes?"[10]

Though Jeffers is himself careful to avoid Barclay's reckless mis-
application of the freedom of God to the human condition, never-
theless it is apparent that its impact upon his spirit is staggering.
An extremely moral man, unbending and nonpermissive by na-
ture, Jeffers's whole psychology is obviously intoxicated with the
awesome significance of God's freedom from choice, from having
to decide, the freedom of being at once Either-Or and Both-And.
It enflames his imagination like liquid fire. It subsumes the con-
dition of all his characters, at times inundating them, dwarfing
them as they struggle with the consequences of what they have
done, overriding their guilts with an irresistable erotic force.
God's apparently indiscriminate incarnational audacity shakes
him:

> Barclay continued not looking downward: "Must he
> love cellular flesh, the hot quivering
> Sheathed fibers, the blood in them,
> And threaded lightning the nerves: had he no choice, are there not
> lions in the nights of Africa
> Roar at his feet under the thunder-cloud manes? Not hawks and
> eagles, the hooked violence between
> The indomitable eyes, storms of carnivorous desire drive over the huge
> blue? He has chosen insanely, he has chosen
> The sly-minded, the cunning-handed, the talkative-mouthed,
> The soft bodies go shelled in cloth: he has chosen to sheathe his power
> in women, sword-strike his passion
> In the eyes of the sons of women. . . . I cannot tell you what madness
> covered him; he heard a girl's voice . . ." Barclay
> Shook like a fire and cried out: "I am not ready to call you.
> Let no one come to me, no one be moved." He stood rigid above them,
> like a man struck blind, feeling
> The spheres of fire rushing through the infinite room in the bubble of
> his mind[11]

Barclay breaks off because in his prophetic vagary he has
touched so deeply the erotic root in the divine that his recent de-

floration of his daughter April rises to silence him. But the truth
will not be hushed. His disciple, the chaste Onorio Vasquez, un-
consciously picks up the theme and innocently articulates it, for
it is irrepressible:

> "The April-eyed, the daughter," he cried in his vision,
> "And the honey of God,
> Walks like a maiden between the hills and high waters,
> She lays her hand passing on the rock at Point Sur,
> The petals of her fingers
> Curve on the black rock's head, the lighthouse with lilies
> Covered, the lightkeepers made drunken like bees
> With her hand's fragrance . . ."[12]

This transmoral freedom of God from the conditions of contin-
gency is of course no new idea. Not only the mystic but the spec-
ulative theologian has anciently insisted on God's infinity of es-
sence, absolutely beyond good and absolutely beyond evil,
utterly transcending every attribute which human conceptualiza-
tion can predicate of Him. But this intuition, always large in the
thought of the most profound religious spirits, is feared and var-
iously eschewed by the masses of men, whether by the supersti-
tious peasantry or the complacent bourgeoisie. Unreflectingly
living by a simplistic identification between God and man, the
truth they could not accept from their saints was eventually
forced upon them by their scientists.

For in the 1920's a host of popular journalists vied with each
other in disabusing the world of its ignorant religious presup-
positions. It was the age of the debunker. Proclaiming that the
amoral god of science left no place for the moral God of religion,
they gloated in their enlightenment, possessing all the freedoms
of the mind and none of the freedoms of the spirit. Few indeed
were untouched by it. In the colleges it was endemic, and even
in the high schools a few hours at the microscope or telescope
persuaded one that the equations of good and evil, the distinction
between assent and denial, seemed pitifully local issues, and
they did not seem large. The Moslem's "There is no God but Al-
lah!" was paraphrased in journalism's "There is no God but
energy." A boy could go wrong, granted—father and mother
and the state might inflict the maximum—but God couldn't care
less.

Yet this universal "scientific" perspective, this pervasive, re-
ductive simplification, was not, actually, the source of Jeffers's ut-
terance. The point is important because his intense academic
training, his adroit scientific vocabulary, and his obvious famil-
iarity with the prevailing generalities of his culture, naturally lead
to that assumption. But even if his philosophy finds its justifi-
cation in the laboratory, his point of view, his *attitude*, originates,
very emphatically, in the more quiveringly primitive root. At bot-
tom it "reeks of religion."

Let us return to *The Idea of the Holy*. We will find that this rig-
orously objective concept of a cosmos of pure power takes us
right back to the beginning of consciousness. There it emerges as
nothing other than the wrath of God. In taking up this basic as-
pect of what he calls the *mysterium tremendum*, Otto makes it clear
that the essence of the idea of the wrath of God lies precisely in
the experience of irresistable force, awesome and impersonal, the
manifestation of what amounts to a detached dreadfulness, reck-
less of human attribution. Here we will be able to verify that what
moves Jeffers derives not from the laboratory but from primitive
religion and stands, actually, behind the credentials of Christian-
ity itself. Otto observes:

But as regards the "wrath of Yahweh," the strange features about it have
for long been a matter for constant remark. In the first place, it is patent
from many passages of the Old Testament that this "wrath" has no con-
cern whatever with moral qualities.

There is something very baffling in the way in which it is kindled, and
manifested. It is, as has been well said, "Like a hidden force of nature,"
like stored up electricity, discharging itself upon anyone who comes too
near.[13]

Perhaps the most famous instance of this is the curious episode
from I Chronicles, 13:7–10, which describes the moving of the
Ark of the Covenant:

And they carried the ark of God in a new cart out of the house of Abin-
abab: and Uzza and Ahio drave the cart.

And David and all Israel played before God with all their might, and
with singing, and with harps, and with psalteries, and with timbrels,
and with cymbals, and with trumpets.

And when they came unto the threshingfloor of Chidon, Uzza put
forth his hand to hold the ark; for the oxen stumbled.

And the anger of the Lord was kindled against Uzza, and he smote him, because he put his hand to the ark; and there he died before God.

Suddenly we seem to be five thousand years ahead with the physicists who, like ancient priests, don their insulating vestments before they enter the laboratory, their holy of holies, to crack the atom.

However, this analogy will not do. Entertaining though it be, the distinctions come thronging in, distinctions as crucial from the religious point of view as from the scientific one. For I believe that Otto, in his concern to emphasize the nonmoral and irrational character of this wrath, does not place his finger on its precise nature, which is, from the religious standpoint, not quite so inexplicable as he assumes. It can be localized in the tension between the Profane and the Sacred. Primitive legends and classical myths abound with instances of this incredible dynamic, which Mircea Eliade characterizes as a "break in plane," the abyss dividing the two modalities of experience. These sources offer many occasions wherein the profane mentality, when introduced by design or by accident into contact with the sacred, or even into its proximity, is overwhelmed by the numinous, or blasted by it, as we have seen with poor Uzza—or as was Acteon, who saw the goddess naked and was torn by hounds. Jeffers draws on this aspect of the wrath when he recalls King Pentheus spying on the god Dionysus, to be torn to pieces by the women followers, among them his own mother.[14] It is the same archetype touched on in *Roan Stallion*, when the profane Johnny overconfidently enters the corral, a confine made sacred by the stallion's breeding, and is struck down. A further instance in which the intrusion of the profane into the sacral order precipitates the outbreak of this wrath is *The Cretan Woman*, an adaptation of the *Hippolytus* of Euripides, wherein the youth, coldly critical of woman, is sacrificed to the indignation of the goddess of love.

Now it goes without saying that many contemporary poets employ such mythical themes, retaining them as one of the standard devices by which the modern sensibility preserves continuity with its past, the roots of our consciousness. Jeffers, however, is not a Symbolist. He sets the teeth of his contemporaries on edge with the solemnity of his direct pronouncement. One is left with the disturbing impression that *this man means it*. And as indicated, the source of our disquietude lies in the very depth of his primitive religious feeling. Eliade throws light on both sides of this ambivalence:

The modern Occidental experiences a certain uneasiness before many manifestations of the sacred. He finds it difficult to accept the fact that, for many human beings, the sacred can be manifested in stones or trees, for example.

But as we shall soon see, what is involved is not a veneration of the stone in itself, a cult of the tree in itself. The sacred tree, the sacred stone are not adored as stone or tree; they are worshipped precisely because they are *hierophanies*, because they show something that is no longer stone or tree but the *sacred*, the *ganz andere*.

It is impossible to overemphasize the paradox represented by every hierophany, even the most elementary. By manifesting the sacred, any object becomes *something else*. Yet it continues to remain itself, for it continues to participate in its surrounding cosmic milieu.

A *sacred* stone remains a *stone*; apparently (or, more precisely, from the profane point of view), nothing distinguishes it from all other stones. But for those to whom a stone reveals itself as sacred, its immediate reality is transmuted into a supernatural reality.

In other words, for those who have a religious experience all nature is capable of revealing itself as cosmic sacrality. The cosmos in its entirety can become a hierophany.[15]

Jeffers, then, is very close to this primal power. For when he evokes the archetype, the divine power concretized in material objects, he is, in the deeps of his creativity, closer to the God of elemental applicative terror than to the more abstract, manageable, and tameable god of energy deduced by nineteenth-century philosophers from the findings of science, and attributed by more than one commentator to the deity celebrated by Jeffers. Actually, his instinct is both more audacious and more menacing.

For instance, in his play *Medea*, he draws directly on the same archetype of the divine numen concretized in a sacerdotal object as that taken above from the Scripture. Medea gives to Jason's bride, as a vengeful wedding present, the cloak which the God of the Sun had presented to her grandfather and which she had retained as a sacred object. Introduced into the egocentric world of Jason and Creon, who between them are sacrificing the latter's daughter to political ambition and the lust for gold, its effect is disastrous. The delighted bride, mindful only of her good fortune, puts on the divine mantle:

> And that doomed girl
> Frightfully crying started up from the chair; she ran, she was like a torch, and the gold crown
> Like a comet streamed fire; she tore at it but it clung to her head; the golden cloak
> Was white-hot, flaying the flesh from the living bones; blood mixed with fire ran down, she fell, she burned
> On the floor, writhing. Then Creon came and flung himself on her, hoping to choke
> That rage of flame, but it ran through him, his own agony
> Made him forget his daughter's. The fire stuck to the flesh, it glued him to her; he tried to stand up,
> He tore her body and his own. The burnt flesh broke
> In lumps from the bones.

The nurse who narrates the divine atrocity covers her eyes with her hands.

> I have finished. They lie there,
> Eyeless, disfaced, untouchable; middens of smoking flesh laced with molten gold . . .[16]

But this is not the end of wrath. The tension between the sacred and the profane drives deeper down, transfers its wrath from the objective action to the very heart, forces Medea to violate her deepest human instinct, her mother's love for her children, compels her to murder her own rather than let them go to the profane, egocentric male. Scholars read this as the conflict in a woman's heart between maternity and jealousy, a jealousy so strong that it triumphs even over maternity. Such is the secular view. At the archetypal level, however, the soul of Medea is founded so deeply upon its primitive sacral base that she cannot see her children sacrificed to the blandness of the profane. She becomes the instrument of the divine wrath. The story is not saying that there is no fury like a woman scorned; it is saying that there is no wrath like divine wrath.

Jeffers makes this clear in his *Solstice*, an earlier treatment of the same myth. Madrone Bothwell, who conforms to the figure of

Medea, confronts her husband, come from the outer world of cities and legality and subsidies to claim the children. He sees their future hopefully, with all the attributes a triumphant secularism can provide:

> "Certainly," he said.
> "They'll live at home with me. They'll have pleasures and advantages
>   you cannot possibly: radio, motion-pictures, books,
> The school, the church. And when they're old enough to go up to
>   college . . ."[17]

Madrone sweeps all this aside, contemptuous and vehement, protesting the very future he dreams for them, a future seen by her only as spiritual ignorance, the omnipresence of the profane:

> What now can save them
> From lives much worse than death, decaying to an average, growing to
>   be like
> All the other insects that fill the cities and defile the country? That
>   listen to imbecile songs and love
> To breathe each other, and eat and drink and make love in common,
>   swarming for pleasure; and from time to time
> A war or a revolution rakes them up like dry straws in a stack and
>   burns them, they hurrah with joy.
> Better the babies die than such lives for them. Do you want them to be
>   like *me*? Do you want them
> To be like *you*?[18]

The sacred reality which she has reserved for her children in death Jeffers situates unerringly in the numinous. It is the same numen that inheres in nature, but he designates it indubitably as divine by the values he sets pulsating there, awakened in his imagery and confirmed in the deep vibrations of his speech:

> It snowed again and the bodies
> were never found. Gopher and ground-squirrel
> And the rooting boar break up the sod in so many places on the high
>   hills. If the children
> Could see from where they lie hidden they'd see
> What a great surf of mountains beats from the distant ocean up to their
>   dwelling-place, wave over wave,
> Waves of live stone; and the low storm-clouds fly through the gorges
>   like hunting eagles. Or if it were summer,

They'd see the quail and the mountain woodpecker walk above them,
    hawks flying, and the great white clouds; they'd see
The sea-fog drawn over the farthest ridges taut as a drum, the dry
    white stream-beds, the strained
Crystal of the air.[19]

In Jeffers's play, Medea stands at the last between powerful ser-
pents, symbols of the unapproachable reality of God, and con-
fronts her stunned beholders, the momentous void of the audi-
ence. In *Solstice* Madrone retires into an equally remote dimen-
sion of the numinous, no less sacral and no less unapproachable:

    Their mother drove east through thickening phantoms
And is thought to have died of thirst in the desert or have killed
    herself, because she was hunted like the last wolf
And never found. Her car was found overturned in a desert gully off
    an abandoned road;
That was perhaps the place where the phantoms caught her; the
    wolf-hunt failed.
I cannot tell; I think she had too much energy to die. I think that a
    fierce unsubdued core
Lives in the high rock in the heart of the continent, affronting the
    bounties of civilization and Christ,
Troublesome, contemptuous, archaic, with thunder-storm hair and
    snowline eyes, *waiting,*
Where the tall Rockies pasture with their heads down, white-spotted
    and streaked like piebald horses, sharp withers
And thunder-scarred shoulders against the sky, standing with their
    heads down, the snow-manes blow in the wind;
But they will lift their heads and whinny when the riders come, they
    will stamp with their hooves and shake down the glaciers.[20]

For of course the wrath of God archetype originates for Jeffers
in the movement of nature, the mystery and terror that informs
it, and in this he is hardly unique. The great poets of Israel felt
much the same way about what they saw of natural violence, and
they celebrated it in verses that have literally drenched the reli-
gious psychology of the West. The Psalms abound with a primi-
tive identification between God and the earth's natural forces,
and whenever these forces exceed man's power, they are expe-
rienced as afflictive. The wrath of God breaks out through them,
and never lets up:

The waters saw thee, O God, the waters saw thee; they were afraid:
the depths also were troubled.
The clouds poured out water: the skies sent out a sound: thine arrows
also went abroad.
The voice of thy thunder was in the heaven; the lightnings lightened
the world; the earth trembled and shook.
Thy way is in the sea, and thy path in the great waters, and thy
footsteps are not known.
Psalm 77: 16–19

Thou didst divide the sea by thy strength: thou brakest the heads of
the dragons in the waters.
Thou brakest the heads of leviathan in pieces, and gavest him to be
meat to the people inhabiting the wilderness.
Thou didst cleave the fountain and the flood: thou driedst up mighty
rivers.
Psalm 74: 13–15

Then the earth shook and trembled; the foundations also of the hills
moved and were shaken, because he was wroth.
There went up a smoke out of His nostrils, and fire out of His mouth
devoured: coals were kindled by it.
He bowed the heavens also and came down: and darkness was under
his feet.
And he rode upon a cherub and did fly: Yea, he did fly upon the wings
of the wind.
He made darkness his secret place; his pavilion round about him were
dark waters and thick clouds of the skies.
At the brightness that was before him his thick clouds passed, hail
stones and coals of fire.
The Lord also thundered in the heavens, and the Highest gave his
voice: hail stones and coals of fire.
Yea, He sent out His arrows, and scattered them; and he shot out
lightnings, and discomfited them.
Then the channels of waters were seen, and the foundations of the
world were discovered at thy rebuke, O Lord, at the blast of the
breath of thy nostrils.
Psalm 18: 7–15

In Jeffers, however, these attributions are not so specific and
never so personalistic as in the way of the Psalmist; there can be
no doubt that with him, also, such violent occurrences, nomi-
nally a process of nature, are always something more. They are
informed with mystery, a manifest supra-natural force, charged

with the numinous, which in the acute consciousness of the poet is palpably assimilated to the wrath. The whole underlying dynamic and intensity of the storm in *Point Sur*'s Prelude is that it is literally freighted with retribution.

But the violence of nature is not only retaliatory, not only a chastisement to man for his profanation of its sacred character, it can be as much a cleansing as a punishment. In fact, the higher octave of the divine vengeance constitutes God's own redemption into purposiveness through the healing it affords. "November Surf" is a perfect example of how the force and threat of natural energies serve the higher purpose of purification:

Some lucky day each November great waves awake and are drawn
Like smoking mountains bright from the west
And come and cover the cliff with white violent cleanness: then
    suddenly
The old granite forgets half a year's filth:
The orange-peel, eggshells, papers, pieces of clothing, the clots
Of dung in the corners of the rock, and used
Sheaths that make light love safe in the evenings: all the droppings of
    the summer
Idlers washed off in a winter ecstasy:
I think this cumbered continent envies its cliff then . . . But all seasons
The earth, in her childlike prophetic sleep,
Keeps dreaming of the bath of a storm that prepares up the long coast
Of the future to scour more than her sea-lines:
The cities gone down, the people fewer and the hawks more
    numerous,
The rivers mouth to source pure; when the two-footed
Mammal, being someways one of the nobler animals, regains
The dignity of room, the value of rareness.[21]

Nor is it storm alone that typifies for Jeffers the divine wrath. Earthquake too serves for its vehicle. Here is an example wherein the violence of earth, as an implicitly retributive divine extension, penetrates into the psychology of the characters. This is from *The Women at Point Sur*:

                    I say that if the mind centers on
        humanity
And is not dulled, but remains powerful enough to feel its own and
    the others, the mind will go mad.

It is needful to remember the stone and the ocean, without the hills
    over the house no endurance,
Without the domed hills and the night. Not for quietness, not peace;
They are moved in their times. Not for repose; they are more strained
    than the mind of a man; tortured and twisted
Layer under layer like tetanus, like the muscles of a mountain bear that
    has gorged the strychnine
With the meat bait: but under their dead agonies, under the nightmare
    pressure, the living mountain
Dreams exaltation; in the scoriac shell, granites and basalts, the reptile
    force in the continent of rock
Pushing against the pit of the ocean, unbearable strains and weights,
    inveterate resistances, dreams westward
The continent, skyward the mountain . . . The old fault
In the steep scarp under the waves
Melted at the deep edge, the teeth of the fracture
Gnashed together, snapping on each other; the powers of the earth
    drank
Their pang of unendurable release and the old resistances
Locked. The long coast was shaken like a leaf.[22]

Now the inspringing of geologic torsion erupts directly into the
psychology and the acts of the protagonists:

    April Barclay
Came from blind lakes of sleep, her mother was laboring
At the locked door, but April in the shaken darkness
Imagined her father breaking entrance and cried out
In a boy's voice, feeling in her hands already
The throat under the beard, but whispering, "Oh, mother,
Don't tremble so." She had slipped from the bed and she felt
The floor under her feet heave and be quieted.
But Audis through her terror had heard the sparrows
Cry out in the oak by the window, in the leonine roar
Of the strained earth, the clatter of bricks or small stones,
And the great timbers of the walls grind on their bearings.[23]

    Often the wrath of God is directly invoked by the characters
themselves, when they have suffered equivocation until it be-
comes unendurable, and, confronting their lives, they beg for
purgation. Tamar declares:

       I have smelled fire and tasted fire,
And all these days of horrible sunlight, fire

Hummed in my ears, I have worn fire about me like a cloak and
    burning for clothing. It is God
Who is tired of the house that thousand-leggers crawl about in, where
    an idiot sleeps beside a ghost-seer,
A doting old man sleeps with dead women and does not know it,
And pointed bones are at the doors
Or climb up trees to the window. I say He has gathered
Fire all about the walls and no one sees it
But I, the old roof is ripe and the rafters
Rotten for burning, and all the woods are nests of horrible things,
    nothing would ever clean them
But fire, but I will go to a clean home by the good river.[24]

And in *The Women at Point Sur*, the girl Faith Herriot invokes
the divine wrath:

        I wish it had shaken the ocean
Over all standing heights and everything alive.
I wish the hills opened their doors and streamed fire, when it struck
    the ankles
The hands would fall in, and when the wrists were burnt through, the
    faces. I wish that it darkened
Toward the last night instead of pinching out the last day
Like a peeled snake.[25]

Then, toward the end of all the appalling action, Natalia catches
up Faith's prayer and echoes her. Convulsed over her own dead
child, she implores:

I wish that the air were sudden poison, and the sun
Blind, and the black sea piled over the mountains.
I wish the wind that roars on the shaking glass
Were a sword in our throats. I wish that the rock
Would spit and vomit, fountains of twisted fire
Catch the spirit with the life: that everything moving
Or feeling between the stars and the center were silent.
That every baby in the world were like this baby.
Take me to the God.[26]

And Fera Martial in *Cawdor* echoes them both:

I wish the little rivers under the laughing kingfishers in every canyon
    were fire, and the ocean
Fire, and my heart not afraid to go down.[27]

And even toward the end of Jeffers's life, in the verse play *The Cretan Woman*, which does not evoke from the poet his greatest powers, one of the few passages that does touch the ancient wellsprings of his poetry is just such a plea from the lips of Phaedra:

> I wish the long black ship that brought me here
> Had split on the sharp reef in the raging storm. I wish my bones were
>   churning unfleshed forever,
> White in black water, out of the sun, wide-washed, far-apart,
>   scattered; and the slime-running seaweed—
> Those cold black leaves—grew where my blood runs—where my heart
>   beats—here in the ribs—here—
> Where your red sword should rest soon.[28]

So, passionately evoked or sent unbeckoned, the wrath breaks out in many ways. For Jeffers, as for primitive man, it serves as the key device in the intensification of religious experience. Whenever human complacency becomes too insular it is always ready to strike open the eyes, reveal the truth within the power that shapes the contour of man's life.

In fact, it is well to reflect that violence, for which Jeffers has been so often rebuked, is for him, as it was for the Biblical prophets, simply a way of liberating the subsistent numen hidden in the context of events, or in the composition of natural objects. Far from being mere destruction, Otto reminds us, " 'Wrath' here is the ideogram of a unique emotional moment in religious experience, a moment whose singularly daunting and awe-inspiring character must be gravely disturbing to those persons who will recognize nothing in the divine nature but goodness, gentleness, love, and a sort of confidential intimacy, in a word, only those aspects of God which turn toward the world of man."[29] We have in this one more clue to the awesome centrality of Jeffers's soul upon primitive religious values. Such contemptuous statements as "under this rain-wind the somber magnificence of the coast / Remembers virtues older than Christ" and "Pride and ferocity are virtues as well as love" must be read as centering on an absolutely fundamental dimension of the religious instinct. Without this recognition, without this *experience*, religions become anemic, cerebral, passionless, effete.

For violence is part of the dynamic of change, springing from a lack of proportion within the multiplicity of things. It is this violence, this wrath, that is divine. Its higher register is the tension between the sacred and the profane, but its lower register inheres in the interior tension subsistent like a vibration in all composites. It is, therefore, ineradicable, and hence inevitable, one of the constitutive elements of reality. Gnosticism seeks by an esoteric formula to sidle between the flanges of violence and emerge unscathed. Buddhism seeks by a strategic withdrawal to elude its crisis, proposing an emergence in a dimension of being where violence does not apply. For the Christian, Christ mounted the Cross, accepted violence into Himself, to place the crucial point precisely where it obtains, the point of convergence between the higher and lower octaves of existence, solving its problem once and for all time.

Sweeping these aside as irrelevant, Jeffers, neither gnostic nor Buddhist nor Christian, nevertheless continues to affirm the religious solution through the force of his unconscious attestation. For no poet can reluct from this centripetal dynamic; in fact the whole estimate of his achievement will be determined by whether or not he takes it full stretch, pushing his principle of formality to the rupture point, or whether he busies himself with verse-formulae, devices which serve as plastic containers rather than weapons which make truth naked. "Poetry," said Robert Frost, "is a way of taking life by the throat." The poetaster is content to take it by the hand.

On every side cries go up at the diffusion and omnipresence of sheer violence in our lives. It permeates our entertainment, our journalism, our art, our dreams—everything save our religion. Yet as a problem it admits of no solution save the religious one, a solution that is itself violent—the last place, actually, our investigators are prepared to look. As the age secularizes and grows "secure," the violence increases. If it does not increase in volume (for it has always been with us), it certainly increases in intensity. The refinements offered by our mass media convert it into the razor's edge, the scalpel that slits, with supreme disinterest, our quivering nerves.

Of all our authors, Jeffers is the one who has most unerringly taken the problem back to its religious roots. Whitman did not

—the attribution of violence remains the central deficiency in his whole perspective. Christian writers do not—preoccupied largely with moral issues, they stress formal, classical, rational solutions. They possess the right symbols but refuse to put them to the test, to push them to the point of fracture, liberate the primitive numen which it is their function to lay bare. Abandoning an inhibitive Christianity to find his religious roots, Jeffers took the violence head on, took it full stretch. He never wearied of it. From first to last he held it to his heart, bore the cosmos of its liberating pain.

In the travail of violence in our literature today, we seek (as men have always sought) resolution through the refinement of aesthetic form. Jeffers does this too, but he goes beyond it. Not despising it but using it, in his best work, wisely and with precision, he yet understands that the tension, the "strain" as he calls it, must be pushed to the point where the numen breaks forth, a strategy constituting what I call the religious solution. Most authors, in a kind of teleological exasperation, precipitate rupture willy-nilly, not to reveal the numen but to flirt with the Void, a tactic of skepticism. That is to say, they press form to the point of fracture but not of revelation. Because they are seeking the Void rather than the numen, their aesthetic captures what they seek. As far as solving the problem of violence goes, they are left with empty hands.

With Jeffers this is rarely so. When it happens that he is left with empty hands, it is not for lack of strategy; it is rather because of his impatience, employing a net of too loose a texture for this particular issue. Otherwise his whole aesthetic, the inclusive deployment of his formal tactic—rough expansiveness of syntax and diction, a stunningly brilliant evocation of image, the karate chop cloture by which imagery is clinched—is to evince, through the application of what can only be called a kind of jagged precision, the central serenity abiding beneath the seethe of conflicting particularities.

Take his poem "Antrim," a brooding response written on his return to the land of his ancestors. Antrim is the northeasternmost county of Ireland, only a few sea-miles from Scotland, where the tides of conflict flowed without stint, shaping the very speech we have inherited, and hence implacably molding modern consciousness itself.

No spot of earth where men have so fiercely for ages of time
Fought and survived and cancelled each other,
Pict and Gael and Dane, McQuillan, Clandonnel, O'Neill,
Savages, the Scot, the Norman, the English,
Here in the narrow passage and the pitiless north, perpetual
Betrayals, relentless resultless fighting.
A random fury of dirks in the dark: a struggle for survival
Of hungry blind cells of life in the womb.
But now the womb has grown old, her strength has gone forth; a few
     red carts in a fog creak flax to the dubs,
And sheep in the high heather cry hungrily that life is hard; a plaintive
     peace; shepherds and peasants.

We have felt the blades meet in the flesh in a hundred ambushes
And the groaning blood bubble in the throat;
In a hundred battles the heavy axes bite the deep bone,
The mountain suddenly stagger and be darkened.
Generation on generation we have seen the blood of boys
And heard the moaning of women massacred,
The passionate flesh and nerves have flamed like pitch-pine and fallen
And lain in the earth softly dissolving.
I have lain and been humbled in all these graves, and mixed new flesh
     with the old and filled the hollow of my mouth
With maggots and rotten dust and ages of repose. I lie here and plot
     the agony of resurrection.[30]

Truly, an excessive poem. But as usual with Jeffers, the subject
itself exceeds in excessiveness anything he can make of it. What
he actually does make of it is the compression of a whole epoch
of conflict into the apotheosis of one surging form, and it is true
in a way that the factuality of no historian could duplicate, be-
cause, as with all great poetry, fact is transmuted into metaphor,
something more holistically faithful than the edifices of specific
detail. This poet knows the dangerously narrow zone that must
be pursued between formality and formlessness, that is, between
the choate and the inchoate, and he takes his chances with an
audacious open form. Shaking his net out with the unerring float-
ing cast of a net-fighter enveloping his prey, he completes the
throw. The quarry is God.

Everything, then, is to the purpose. In his narratives the self-
inflictions of his characters are not the acts of "emotional mech-
anisms, lewd and twitching conglomerations of plexi, their hu-

manity annulled," as Yvor Winters has it.[31] They are attempts to touch to the impoverished civilized self the numen which violence releases, and so to achieve purgation. Over and over Jeffers situates these incidents in the context of natural grandeur and makes it obvious that the numen in the strained elements and the numen in the strained flesh respond to and support each other, give each their religious identity. With the house-burning at the bloody close of *Hungerfield*,

> The stream and the deep-throated waves of the ocean glittered with
>   crimson lightnings, and the low cloud
> Gaped like a lion's mouth, swallowing the flights of flame and the soul
>   of a man. It is thus (and will be) that violence
> Turns on itself, and builds on the wreck of violence its violent beauty,
>   the spiring fire-fountain
> And final peace: grim in the desert in the lion's carcass the hive of
>   honey.[32]

God cries through the gash, the rupture in natural self-sufficience, reclaiming His own, that which He created, in the prime, jealous of its purity of conception. In the denouement of *Thurso's Landing*, of all Jeffers's work the one that most nearly approximates the terminal resolution of Elizabethan drama, the poet releases one survivor out of three, and declares:

>   The platform is like a rough plank
>   theater-stage
> Built on the brow of the promontory: as if our blood had labored all
>   round the earth from Asia
> To play its mystery before strict judges at last, the final ocean and sky,
>   to prove our nature
> More shining than that of the other animals. It is rather ignoble in its
>   quiet times, mean in its pleasures,
> Slavish in the mass; but at stricken moments it can shine terribly
>   against the dark magnificence of things.[33]

For it is at such "stricken moments," the point of crisis, that human freedom is most manifest, that the spiritual principle is liberated from the fatality of the material continuum. The saint and the artist *create* their points of crisis in order to call that freedom into being. The real failures in life are those unable to create at all—who are, in the drama of existence, neither saints nor artists.

A great deal of their violence is due to haphazard attempts to pre-
cipitate crisis willy-nilly, seeking to create potential threshold ex-
periences, to effect somehow the apertures of release. As artists
or saints they are simply inept, these assassins, terrorists, mur-
derers, rioters. Unable to fulfill the criteria truly constituting a
peak experience, they leave us, their unwilling audience, sick-
ened and unfulfilled.

It has remained for Jeffers, in his astonishing naiveté, in his un-
spoiled religious simplicity, to push the solution to its existential
limit, make it "shine terribly against the dark magnificence of
things." In this he becomes a kind of priest of the word, who of-
fers to the gods sacrificial victims that the people may be purged.
Early in our Protestant culture, this function was taken up pri-
vately in the devout reading of Scripture, where the violence and
the wrath conjoined to reveal the numen in the darker glory.
With the decline of Scripture reading and of verse, and the cor-
responding rise of a prose sensibility, the subsistent religious nu-
men vanished into the Void, and men were content to leave it
there, appeasing their *angst* with intellectual consolations, a self-
congratulatory doubt. Now the violence seeps out of the Void and
floods back into life. Too late for either poetry or the hasty revival
of Scripture reading to contain it, it strangles us with wrath.

Looking back on it, surrounded by the violence we cannot con-
tain, we can see how crucial in Scripture was the conjoining of
sacred history and the appropriation of violence into the dimen-
sion of ultimate meanings. And it was done not only through the
primitivistic irruptions of the Old Testament, but also through
the eschatological anticipations of the New Testament. Actually,
the divine violence finds its apogeic consummation in the book
that closes the entire panorama of salvation history. "The Apoc-
alypse," it has been written, "is a vision of violence—the most
extreme, the most unrelieved violence to be found in the whole
of the Bible."[34] It is almost as if the farther we proceed in the evo-
lution of spiritual awareness, the more resoundingly beats upon
the shores of our consciousness the ocean of divine wrath. By
a correspondingly processive law, the more sensitive we be-
come, the more shattering the impact of that wrath upon our
mentality.

It is not my purpose here to claim for Jeffers the rarefied spiritual elevation of the great mystics and contemplatives, to whose witness the history of religion so eloquently attests. Rather, I seek only to establish a point of some significance. It is well known that Jeffers personally was so intolerably sensitive to pain that he could not bear to inflict it. George Sterling had to bring a rifle to Tor House to stem an invasion of ground squirrels, the little rodents Jeffers was incapable of killing. The same commentator who cited the Apocalypse above lets us know that what was operative in the twentieth-century poet was very probably true of the first-century saint, that violent book's author:

It is perhaps worth remembering that the Apostle who saw this, and who wrote down what he saw, was the Apostle of Love, the disciple whom Jesus loved; not the rash Peter, not that blacksmith of the Lord, Paul. But the gentle John. He who loved most, to whom after Our Lord's death it was given to look after the Blessed Virgin Mary, the reserved, domestic John—so one thinks of him, as a retiring figure, a kind of Newman, etherealized, a creature of light and philosophy, a lover, possibly, of music—he it is who sees most appalling visions.[35]

What is the principle by which life's most retiring and painfully sensitive men promulgate the most violent of visions?

We must not confuse the spiritual eye with the eye of flesh and blood. We must not confuse a vision of violence with the behavior of violence. These things are opposites; they go by contraries. The thug does not have violent visions. He has no vision at all. With his inner eye he sees nothing. Blindly, destructively, he spreads violence all around him. It is those who stay at home who see the most.[36]

Jeffers stayed home. But what he beheld in his mind's eye, turned inward upon the deeps of his nature, and outward upon the beauty of God in the vast cosmos that spread about him, was the wrath that shakes the universe on its hinges and rebukes our pride with every glint of prime being.

II. THE RACE-NAUGHTING

The essence of the radical mentality lies in its need and in its capacity to define itself emphatically over against the prevalent social and institutional assumptions of its time. Its function is to counterbalance severe but unrecognized deficiencies in the body politic and thereby to compensate for grave threats to the future of the race that follow in the wake of society's monolithic inertia. As the radical speaks out, he generates an extremeness of expression proportionate to his alienation from the normative conventions, conventions that have lost contact with true interiority and have become dangerously solidified at more superficial collective levels, no longer enjoying contact with the living roots that gave them birth.

In religion this radical mentality takes two forms—the prophetic and the mystical. Traditionally, the prophetic voice indicts the inertia of the institutional as it gravitates toward the grip of materialistic and sensual complacencies. The mystical voice, on the other hand, is not directed toward the collective. It is the voice of the visionary suffering in his alienation from God, and the extremity of his expression takes on a corresponding intensity as his sense of alienation deepens. But in both cases what is in play is the radical mentality in its historic role of readjustment between opposed polarities—the Absolute and the Collective on the one hand, and the Absolute and the Self on the other.

In Jeffers we see both forms of this radical consciousness, but it is my belief that we see them combined in a manner that is unique. If it is true that we see them *in potentia* in every radical spirit—and no better example need be sought than the ordeal and dilemma of Moses caught as no one before or since has been caught, save Christ alone, between a majestic God and an errant people—I think it is safe to say that Jeffers has developed the dilemma along lines that are unprecedented in visionary radical thought.

In order to set the problem in its proper mystical dimension, let us go on with Otto to consider the further extension of the concept of "absolute overpoweringness."

We will take to represent this the term *majestas*, majesty—the more readily because anyone with a feeling for language must detect a last faint trace of the numinous still clinging to the word. The tremendum by then may be rendered more adequately *tremendum majestas*, or "aweful majesty."[37]

He then goes on to localize this ingredient more specifically in the vaster element of the numinous as it relates to mysticism:

This second element of majesty may continue to be vividly preserved, where the first, that of unapproachability, recedes and dies away, as may be seen, for example, in mysticism. It is especially in relation to this element of majesty or absolute overpoweringness that the creature-consciousness, of which we have already spoken, comes upon the scene, as a sort of shadow or subjective reflection of it. Thus, in contrast to the "overpowering" of which we are conscious as an object over against the self, there is the feeling of one's own submergence, of being but dust and ashes and *nothingness*. And this forms the numinous raw material for the feeling of religious humility.[38]

Otto carefully distinguishes this sense of religious humility from that other sense of createdness, namely, profound gratitude for existence. By contrast, what he here seeks to isolate carries an entirely different weight:

We come upon the ideas, first, of the annihilation of self, and then, as its complement, of the transcendent as the sole and entire reality. These are the characteristic notes of mysticism in all its forms, however otherwise various in content. For one of the chief tests and most general features of mysticism is just this *self-depreciation*, the estimation of the self, of the personal "I" as something not perfectly or essentially real, or even as mere nullity, a self-depreciation which comes to demand its own fulfillment, in practice, in rejecting the delusion of selfhood, and so makes for the annihilation of the self.[39]

Here we approach what will be recognized as a fundamental aspect of Jeffers's thought, but it must be instantly added that while on some occasions he does take the attitude of personal mysticism in its historic sense of self-naughting, it is far more often that he incorporates it within his prophetic role and applies it to humanity as a whole. And this is his contribution, at least in modern expression, to the historic problem. Here too so much protest and so many rebukes against him find their point of origin. But it is apparent that this protest and these rebukes proceed from a lack of perspective as to his mystical presuppositions. Carpenter well notes:

To describe Jeffers' poetic Inhumanism in terms of mysticism is to suggest an explanation of many poetic attitudes which have seemed merely personal or perverse. His denunciation of humanity is repeated by many mystics who have desired to produce a "realizing sense of sin" and a resulting detachment from the affairs of this world. So Plotinus sought in the mystical experience a "liberation from all terrene concerns . . . a

flight of the alone to the alone." The poet mystic would cut humanity
from his system in order to free himself to fall in love with God.[40]

Now Jeffers's race-naughting, the mystic's traditional and per-
sonal self-naughting applied to the human race as a whole, has
come about by virtue of the triumph of collective consciousness
over nature and its processes, so that humanity seeks unity not
in reference to the greater reality of the divine Other, as in sacral
cultures, but rather in its self-obsession with its own preoccu-
pations, the keynote of our secular life. Jeffers, then, by virtue of
his historical position, may well be the first religious visionary
methodically to formulate and massively to register this break
and extension of self-naughting to the race, the shift from indi-
vidual consciousness to collective consciousness. We have al-
ready seen how Jeffers used the device of reduction to touch the
feeling of creature-consciousness. There, creature-consciousness
was itself intensified to the point of race-naughting, and in-
stances of the one will serve for the other. But his mystical intu-
ition is obsessed by it and returns to it constantly, as in the fol-
lowing passage from "Margrave":

> The learned astronomer
> Analyzing the light of most remote star-swirls
> Has found them—or a trick of distance deludes his prism—
> All at incredible speeds fleeing outward from ours.
> I thought, no doubt they are fleeing the contagion
> Of consciousness that infects this corner of space.
> · · ·
> So, I thought, the rumor
> Of human consciousness has gone abroad in the world,
> The sane uninfected far-outer universes
> Flee it in a panic of escape, as men flee the plague
> Taking a city
> · · ·
> You would be wise, you far stars,
> To flee with the speed of light this infection.
> For here the good sane invulnerable material
> And nature of things more and more grows alive and cries.
> The rock and water grow human, the bitter weed
> Of consciousness catches the sun, it clings to the near stars,
> Even the nearer portion of the universal God
> Seems to become conscious, yearns and rejoices

And suffers: I believe this hurt will be healed
Some age of time after mankind has died,
Then the sun will say "What ailed me a moment?" and resume
The old soulless triumph, and the iron and stone earth
With confident inorganic glory obliterate
Her ruins and fossils, like that incredible unfading red rose
Of desert in Arizona glowing life to scorn,
And grind the chalky emptied seed-shells of consciousness
The bare skulls of the dead to powder; after some million
Courses around the sun her sadness may pass:
But why should you worlds of the virgin distance
Endure to survive what it were better to escape?[41]

Then Jeffers seizes the mystic's traditional self-naughting to en-
force this other naughting, and throws self-indictment into the
balance to deepen his polarity of vision:

I also am not innocent
Of contagion, but have spread my spirit on the deep world.
I have gotten sons and sent the fire wider.
I have planted trees, they also feel while they live.
I have humanized the ancient sea-sculptured cliff
And the ocean's wreckage of rock
Into a house and a tower,
Hastening the sure decay of granite with my hammer,
Its hard dust will make soft flesh;
And have widened in my idleness
The disastrous personality of life with poems,
That are pleasant enough in the breeding but go bitterly at last
To envy oblivion and the early deaths of nobler
Verse, and much nobler flesh.
And I have projected my spirit
Behind the superb sufficient forehead of nature
To gift the inhuman God with this rankling consciousness.

But who is our judge? It is likely the enormous
Beauty of the world requires for completion our ghostly increment,
It has to dream, and dream badly, a moment of its night.[42]

So the race-naughting is resumed, as if Jeffers realized that too
much self-naughting will compromise his essential mission,
which is not to show himself to himself, but to show the human
race to itself. And, as in these lines from "Thebaid," he carries it
to the strange extremes that are the opposite of self-naughting,

that have in fact brought upon him charges of inflation, ego-
mania, and worse.

> Hermit from stone cell
> Gazing with great stunned eyes,
> What extravagant miracle
> Has amazed them with light,
> What visions, what crazy glory, what wings?
> —I see the sun set and rise
> And the beautiful desert sand
> And the stars at night,
> The incredible magnificence of things.
> I the last living man
> That sees the real earth and skies,
> Actual life and real death.
> The others are all prophets and believers
> Delirious with fevers of faith.[43]

The real prophet stops at nothing to confront the race to itself so
that it might turn from itself and love God. Furthermore, the lines
carry something other than they are thought to carry—the intol-
erable loneliness of the religious spirit utterly isolated by the stu-
pendous truth of its vision.

For as Otto goes on to say, the other side of that self-naughting
of the mystic is the insight into the transcendence of the Reality
against which the subject is gauged, and its final warrant of
existence.

And on the other hand mysticism leads to a valuation of the transcen-
dent object of its reference as that which through plenitude of being
stands supreme and absolute, so that the finite self contrasted with it
becomes conscious even in its nullity that "I am naught, Thou are all."
There is no thought in this of any causal relation between God, the Cre-
ator, and the self, the creature. The point from which speculation starts
is not a "consciousness of absolute dependence"—not myself as result
and effect of a divine cause—for that would in point of fact lead to insis-
tence upon the reality of the self. It starts from a consciousness of the
absolute superiority or supremacy of a power other than myself, and it
is only as it falls back upon ontological terms to achieve its end—terms
generally borrowed from natural science—that the element of the *tre-
mendum*, originally apprehended as "plenitude of power," becomes
transmuted into "plenitude of being."[44]

It is this voice, the voice of divine self-sufficiency and plenitude speaking in the language of natural science, that we clearly see in Barclay's vision from *The Women at Point Sur*:

> The God in his mind answered,
> "These also return."
> It seemed to Barclay the cloud broke and he saw the stars.
> Those of this swarm were many, but beyond them universe past
>   universe
> Flared to infinity, no end conceivable. Alien, alien, alien universes. At
>   length, one similar
> To this one; instantly his mind crying through the vastness
> Pitched on the twin of this one, the intolerable identical
> Face framed in the same disastrous galaxy: and if once repeated
> Repeated forever. He heard the scream of suffered violence on the dark
>   hill; he ate the miracle,
> The closed serpent.
> Consciousness drowned and sleep covered him.[45]

We encounter this voice at its most awesome and fulfilled level in the utterance of the Hanged God in "At the Birth of an Age":

> Pain and their endless cries. How they cry to me: but they are I: let
>   them ask themselves.
> I am they, and there is nothing beside. I am alone and time passes,
>   time also is in me, the long
> Beat of this unquiet heart, the quick drip of this blood, the whirl and
>   returning waves of the stars,
> The course of this thought.
> My particles have companions and happy fulfillments, each star has
>   stars to answer him and hungry night
> To take his shining, and turn it again and make it a star; each beast has
>   food to find and his mating,
> And the hostile and helpful world; each atom has related atoms, and
>   hungry emptiness around him to take
> His little shining cry and cry it back; but I am all, the emptiness and
>   all, the shining and the night.
> All alone, I alone.[46]

Thus, plenitude of power transmuted into plenitude of being and trembling in the mystic's gaze becomes the voice of exalted poetry.

For all its exaltation, however, the intense tone, the pitch of utterance, denotes here the radical mentality in its extremity of situation, confirming the presence of the prophet and the mystic, each in their historic roles caught in a single creative mentality, each trying to do justice to the office inherent in its point of view, and each well-nigh canceling the other out, in the mystic's vision before the unutterable, but no less so in the prophet's dilemma, incommunicable with a people blind with spiritual ignorance. The stretch and magnitude of his attempt are the signature of Jeffers's place as a visionary poet—prophet and mystic subsumed in the calling of one who, however he sees and however he feels, is nothing unless he can at last find voice, aware as he is that, in the presence of such magnitudes, to utter is to fail.

III. THE WHOLLY OTHER

"Nothing," writes Robert Martin Adams, beginning his study of the nineteenth-century literary conquest of the Void, "nothing is closer to the supreme commonplace of our commonplace age than its preoccupation with Nothing." What he has in mind is our "elected experience of, and deliberate exploitation of" that concept, which may be "un-self-conscious non-experience" in one sense, but in another is "willful submission of oneself to non-experience as an active form of experience."[47] He goes on to list some of the multitudinous manifestations that characterize the expression of this pursuit today. These include various kinds of experiments dealing with weightlessness, silence, and interruption of the sense-continuum which have captured the imagination of the time; exhibitions of framed blank canvas; and musical compositions which consist of total silence. This preoccupation also is addressed in more serious ways:

The philosopher who speaks most closely to the contemporary condition is Jean-Paul Sartre, whose preoccupation with Nothingness and the pressures it brings to bear on men is too well known to need documenting. Kenneth Burke makes man's capacity for negation one of only four elements in his essential definition of humanity. Freud sees negation as an essential screen behind which repressed material can rise to consciousness; this psychological mechanism gives another content to the assertion in Hegel's *Phenomenology* that the force of negation and negativity, the pressure of nay-saying, is that which not only defines the self but enables it to rise to self-consciousness and true freedom. More a fad than a serious philosophy, at least in the West, Zen Buddhism invites one to perceive objects out of all intellectual context, as unique, immediate, unverbalizable presences; its highest objective is to liberate the mind completely from bondage to things, so that it may seek its proper freedom in the realm of Nothing.[48]

The list goes on for two more pages, and concludes, not unreasonably, "The basic point needs no arguing. In art, in literature, in science, in our culture as a whole, we are a void-haunted, void-fascinated age."[49]

These reflections serve to introduce us to one aspect of the thought of Robinson Jeffers which not only establishes him within the mainstream of his time, but also serves sharply to demarcate him from it. For if the charge against him is, as so often it has been, that of negation, how is it that negation is the basic subject matter and the recurrent theme of almost all the creators of our literature? How can he, in his preoccupation with the negative, be so much in the mainstream and yet, in his treatment, in his solutions, be so far outside it?

Yet it is so. And being so, this can only mean that negation itself is not an absolute concept but must have a variety of facets, its own distinctions and equivocations, dependent upon our attitude and on the salience of the engaged mind. Adams's study of the practice of negation in the nineteenth century is an effort to throw light on this problem, which, if not at the source in our culture, is at least sufficiently far back to provide us with the perspective necessary to get it in focus. But since Jeffers can find no root among these immediate ancestors, it appears that the subject yields even deeper distinctions than such modern aspects of it have afforded. Let us, therefore, go to a more basic text for clarification.

Mircea Eliade, in his study *The Sacred and the Profane*, distinguishes sharply between the "religious man" of the archaic and traditional societies and the "nonreligious man" of the modern world. Of the former he writes:

As we said before, religious man assumes a particular and characteristic mode of existence in the world, and despite the great number of historico-religious forms, this characteristic mode is always recognizable. Whatever the historic context in which he is placed, *homo religiosus* always believes that there is an absolute reality, *the sacred*, which transcends this world but manifests itself in this world, thereby sanctifying it and making it real. He further believes that life has a sacred origin and that human existence realizes all of its potentialities in proportion as it is religious—that is, participates in reality.[50]

Now it is apparent that Jeffers fits decisively within this context. To participate in reality by virtue of its divine character is the central theme of his testament. Transcendence as the mode of ultimate realization is the basic program of all he advocates. If this is so, no less evident is his radical distinction from "nonreligious man," as Eliade defines him:

It is easy to see all that separates this mode of being in the world from the existence of nonreligious man. First of all, the nonreligious man refuses transcendence, accepts the relativity of "reality" and may even come to doubt the meaning of existence. The great cultures of the past too have not been entirely without nonreligious men, and it is not impossible that such men existed even on the archaic levels of culture, although as yet no testimony to their existence there has come to light. But it is only in the modern societies of the West that nonreligious man has developed fully. Modern nonreligious man assumes a new existential situation; he regards himself solely as the subject and agent of history, and he refuses all appeal to transcendence. In other words, he accepts no model for humanity outside the human condition as it can be seen in the various historical situations. Man *makes himself,* and he only makes himself completely in proportion as he desacralizes himself and the world. The sacred is the prime obstacle to his freedom. He will become himself only when he is totally demysticized. He will not be truly free until he has killed the last god.[51]

By these terms, Robinson Jeffers is not a modern man. In this sketch, in which we can recognize so many of our writers and intellectuals, we can detect all that excludes Jeffers from the mainstream of his time—and this despite his preoccupation with the negative. For it is apparent that these two basic points of view, constituting as they do two diametrically opposed attitudes to the phenomenal world, are going to obtain with no less force when confronting the Void. The basic psychological method of religious man is faith, whereas that of nonreligious man is skepticism.

Now it is generally believed that skepticism is a sort of historical by-product of the disappearance of religious faith. Actually, as we saw from Eliade, it is a deliberate creation of the mind (unconsciously conceived, true, but no less deliberate for all that) in order to annul the aura of faith that sustained it. For "the sacred is the prime obstacle to his freedom." As such, it must go, and skepticism is the tool that will accomplish it. It is the psychological method by which profane man will secure the sovereignty of reason over faith as the essential intellectual mode of his existence.

From this it is apparent that the contemporary preoccupation with the Void is the end product of the skeptical method. It is occasioned by a crisis of the intelligence as it exhausts the extensive possibilities consequent upon the attainment of its cultural objectives. The objective was, nominally, the mastery of phenomena in order to secure freedom. But the method, no less than the objective, was instrumental to the present confrontation with the Void, for it is the prolongation of the method which renders unenjoyable the rewards of the objective, the manifest freedom gained. The method was skeptcism, and skepticism destroys its objectives no less totally than the obstacles to freedom it attacked. It is the attack of skepticism on the Void that is destroying intelligence itself.

If nonreligious man, confronting the Void, is left with a monumental, self-reflective impasse, what is the situation of religious man when the Void looms? What becomes of his method, and does he experience any progression? If so, does this progression constitute a kind of liberty that denotes a superiority over the freedom of nonreligious man? (For the freedom of skepticism is indeed verified in negation.) Does each provide a different kind of freedom? And is the freedom of faith, insofar as it admits of progression, a true freedom? And is the freedom of skepticism, insofar as it encounters an ultimate impasse, a freedom that is false?

I do not believe these questions admit, as yet, of demonstrable solutions, for the concepts of faith and skepticism are, as yet, too conditioned by their European background, too much a part of the post-Christian historical situation. Rather, in order to get on with the problem of Robinson Jeffers, I propose to compare and contrast him with the normative pattern by reverting to the prior question from which the others evolved—namely, what is the situation of religious man when the Void looms? In order to do so, let us return to Otto and *The Idea of the Holy*, where we left him in his analysis of the *mysterium tremendum*.

Turning in his analysis of numinous properties from the *tremendum* to the *mysterium*, Otto discerns two elements, the "wholly other" and the "fascinans." With respect to the wholly other, the key term is the word *stupor*, which denotes the affective state precipitated by the apprehension of the wholly other. Says Otto:

> *Stupor* is plainly a different thing from *tremor*; it signifies blank wonder, an astonishment that strikes us dumb, amazement absolute. . . . The truly "mysterious" object is beyond our apprehension and comprehension, not only because our knowledge has certain irremovable limits, but because in it we come upon something inherently "wholly other," whose kind and character are incommensurable with our own and before which we therefore recoil in a wonder that strikes us chill and numb.[52]

Here, we realize, we are at the threshold of the Void that is the preoccupation of modern man. Now Otto shows that in mysticism we have in the "beyond" the strongest stressing and overstressing of those nonrational elements which are already inherent in all religion. Mysticism pursues to its extreme point this contrasting of the numinous, the numen experienced as the wholly other, with ordinary experience:

> Not content with contrasting it with all that is of nature or this world, mysticism concludes by contrasting it with Being itself and all that "is," and finally actually calls it "that which is nothing." By this "nothing" is meant not only that which is absolutely and intrinsically other than and opposite of everything that is and can be thought. But while exaggerating to the point of paradox this *negation* and contrast—the only means open to conceptual thought to apprehend the *mysterium*—mysticism at the same time retains the *positive quality* of the "wholly other" as a very living factor in its over-brimming religious emotion.[53]

We can understand in this how that quality in the thought of religious man can be seen as radically different from the concept of negation in the skeptical man. We are also able to understand that until Jeffers is seen as a mystic rather than a philosopher, the ambiguities and paradoxes with which he wrestles admit of no satisfactory conclusion. As mysticism, however, all becomes clear:

But what is true of the strange "nothingness" of our mystics holds good equally of the *sunyam* and the *sunyata*, the "void" and "emptiness" of the Buddhist mystics. This aspiration for the "void" and for becoming void, no less than the aspiration of our western mystics for "nothing" and for becoming nothing, must seem a kind of lunacy to anyone who has no inner sympathy for the esoteric language and ideographs of mysticism, and lacks the matrix from which these come necessarily to birth. To such an one Buddhism itself will be simply a morbid sort of pessimism. But in fact the "void" of the eastern, like the "nothing" of the western mystic, is a numinous ideogram of the "wholly other."[54]

We are in this clearly able to distinguish the preoccupation with the Void as seen from a mystical experience and the same preoccupation with that other Void which reveals not the emptiness of God but the emptiness of intelligence. Otto pursues further the thread of negation that runs all through the positive of religion and explains why it must be.

The terms "supernatural" and "transcendental" give the appearance of positive attributes, and, as applied to the mysterious, they appear to divest the *mysterium* of its originally negative meaning and to turn it into an affirmation. On the side of conceptual thought this is nothing more than appearance, for it is obvious that the two terms in question are merely negative and exclusive attributes with reference to "nature" and the world of cosmos respectively. But on the side of the feeling-content it is otherwise; that *is* in very truth positive in the highest degree, though here too, as before, it cannot be rendered explicit in conceptual terms. It is through this positive feeling-content that the concepts of the "transcendent" and "supernatural" become forthwith designations for a unique "wholly other" reality and quality, something of whose special character we can *feel*, without being able to give it clear conceptual expression.[55]

We are here at the breakover point that distinguishes transcendental negation from the negation of skepticism. The latter attacks the datum of the feelings no less ruthlessly than any other element of the phenomenal world—in fact more ruthlessly, for the skeptic cannot, in principle, trust these intuitions, because to do so would confirm his bondage to the "sacral," which he set out to eliminate in order to secure his freedom. To the religious man, however, these intuitions are the emphatic witness of his feeling, verify the force and quality of his feeling-state and constitute the

guarantee of its excellence and authority. This enables him to con-
front the Void conceptually, maintaining a secure base in the
emotions.

With these considerations before us, we are able to see why Jef-
fers, despite his engagement of the Void as the primary concern
of his verse, stands outside the mainstream of that other con-
frontation which constitutes the keynote of modern man. But it
also enables us to refute those other critics who, committed to a
moral solution to the problem of the Void, accuse him of nihilism.

For instance, the great emphasis on "annihilation" in *The
Women at Point Sur*, which brought down upon him such charges,
must surely emerge in a more positive light. Everywhere,
through feeling-states marvelously evoked in language, Jeffers
affirms the positive element in the annihilative principle he proj-
ects. Because he does not use traditional mystical terminology,
either Western or Eastern, commentators have been led to attrib-
ute a purely phenomenological contour to his writings, chiefly
since he has worked his way into these mystical states through a
substratum of scientific thought and imagery rather than through
a mystical or metaphysical one.

Actually, from the religious point of view, his value for us
would seem in this instance to lie in the fact that he *rediscovers* the
basic mystical constituents as Otto has laid them forth. The tra-
ditional mystical program, which, as a lapsed Christian, he might
have been familiar with, must have existed in his mind only at a
superficial, or merely cultural level, acquired casually from his
general reading, but remaining unfocused because of his nominal
disinterest in traditional religious structures or hegemonies. His
fascination was science. But by virtue of his intensely religious
nature and his poetic commitment, his thirst for the absolute
forced him to push forward beyond the bounds of science or po-
etry, and so in the end he discovered himself at the mystic's an-
cient and traditional situation.

In *Tamar* he thrust to the obverse side of morality, pushing the
principle of consciousness beyond the normative strictures that
serve initially to define it. Tamar, sexually tempting her father,
declares:

> I'll show you your trouble, you
> sinned, your old book calls it, and repented: that was foolish.

I was unluckier, I had no chance to repent, so I learned something, we
    must keep sin pure
Or it will poison us, the grain of goodness in a sin is poison. Old man,
    you have no conception
Of the freedom of purity. Lock the door[56]

In *The Tower Beyond Tragedy*, Jeffers pursued the quest through the
interstices of phenomena ever more deeply:

> I entered the life of the brown forest
> And the great life of the ancient peaks, the patience of stone, I felt the
>   changes in the veins
> In the throat of the mountain, a grain in many centuries, we have our
>   own time, not yours; and I was the stream
> Draining the mountain wood; and I the stag drinking; and I was the
>   stars,
> Boiling with light, wandering alone, each one the lord of his own
>   summit; and I was the darkness
> Outside the stars, I included them, they were a part of me. I was
>   mankind also, a moving lichen
> On the cheek of the round stone . . . they have not made words for it,
>   to go behind things, beyond hours and ages,
> And be all things in all time, in their returns and passages, in the
>   motionless and timeless center,
> In the white of the fire . . . how can I express the excellence I have
>   found, that has no color but clearness;
> No honey but ecstasy; nothing wrought nor remembered; no
>   undertone nor silver second murmur
> That rings in love's voice, I and my loved are one; no desire but
>   fulfilled; no passion but peace,
> The pure flame and the white, fierier than any passion; no time but
>   spheral eternity[57]

It is the sense and quality of original discovery that gives these
words their freshness, and if the germ of truth in them is identical
with the ancient tradition of mysticism, I believe nonetheless that
the energy of the utterance is sourced in the freshness of revela-
tion. But that is the essence of mysticism: every moment is dis-
covered as something utterly new.

    Yet it was in *The Women at Point Sur* that Jeffers pushed his lan-
guage to the point of breakthrough and discovered the word that
would most deeply shape the roots of his thought: annihilation.
Annihilation constitutes the obliteration of all phenomena in or-

der to arrive at the essence of what truly is. Barclay, early in the
narrative, stumbles almost by chance on the conceptual possibil-
ities lurking in the word. Significantly, just as in *Tamar* it is in the
presence of the sin of incest that the opportunity occurs, so Bar-
clay recalls his rage when his son and daughter locked them-
selves in the bedroom to say goodbye to each other on the eve of
the young man's departure for war:

That anger of his when Edward before his departure
Locked himself in the room with April to bid her farewell:
He had paced the hallway below, his mind boiling,
And suffered like a fainting fit or a dizziness:
Sorrow at his son's departure: annihilating the world
A moment or more.[58]

It is at this point that the possibilities latent in violation (Tamar's
"You have no conception of the freedom of purity"), begin to
dawn on him:

        Annihilation, the beautiful
Word, the black crystal structure, prisms of black crystal
Arranged the one behind the other in the word
To catch a ray not of this world.[59]

All Barclay's violational acts were simply "prisms of black crystal"
to reach the ray beyond the concept, the essential flick beyond
violation. At the end, Barclay bends above his daughter's self-
destroyed body:

                    He smelled the gun's breath and
    lifted his face
Into abstract existence: consciousness abstracted from feeling; the
    wires of pain-pleasure
Burned out, the ways of consciousness cleared perfectly.
Himself was the desert that he had entered; these millions of millions
Were grains of sand of himself, all present, all counted,
All known. The thing can hardly be spoken further. April was dead:
But all that passion a fable: had served the purpose.
The dead have ears but no mouths, one's like another.
They are grains of sand on the sand; the living are grains of sand on
    the wind; the wind crying "I want nothing,"
Neither hot nor cold, raging across the sands, not shifting a point,
Wanting *nothing*: annihilation's impossible, the dead have none: it
    wants, actively, *nothing*[60]

The concept is pushed in the mad minister's mind even one step further: "Annihilation's impossible, the unborn have none."

When Mark Van Doren said of this poem that Jeffers seemed to be knocking his head against the night, it was true, but what he was discovering in that attempt was the *nada* mystics had always engaged and come to know. The point is important because it makes all the difference whether a poet is hopelessly aberrant, or whether he is resolutely pursuing a vision through the opening of new poetic perspectives, authentic probes to the roots of consciousness.

Toward the end of his career, after the atom bomb had confronted the world with its own prospect of the Void, and after the passion of discovery had somewhat abated, Jeffers once again reflected on emptiness, more or less in passing, but sufficiently to let us know that he had pretty much come to terms with its problem for himself. In the nameless old man who is the protagonist of the quasi-fabulous morality play *The Inhumanist*, a character Jeffers has created to serve as the image of man at his possible best as Jeffers conceives of him, he introduces an incident that is of interest to us because it is also an encounter between the sacred and profane attitudes as we saw them in the discussion of the wrath of God. The old man with his mythical double axe, a hierophany that sings and screams in the presence of untruth, encounters a fugitive scientist who has perfected a secret formula which will permit the creation of an enormously fatal weapon, but who now refuses to transmit its code out of distrust of the purposes to which it will be put. Fleeing to the Big Sur coast in search of sanctuary, he professes the disinterested abstract purity of science, a mode of the mind superior to any practical application:

> "So I have cheated," he said, "the American
>   Army and am run away.
> Science is not a chambermaid-woman." "Brother," the old man said,
>   "you are right.
> Science is an adoration; a kind of worship." "So?" he said,
> "Worship?" His round blue eyes behind the bright glasses grew
>   opaque and careful:
> "What then is worship?" The old man considered him and said slowly:
>   "A contemplation of God." "*Das noch!*" he answered,

"*Das fehlte noch!* I am a man who thought that even old peasants and
　　leather cowboys after this war
Had learned something." "A coming nearer to God," the old man said
　　slowly. "To learn his ways
And love his beauty." "*Ja, so,*" he said, "*der uralte Bloedsinn.* I hope the
　　Russians
Destroy you and your God."[61]

Confronted with the profane, the sacral registers the primal re-
action of the archaic and undilutable wrath of God:

　　　　　　　　　　　　　　Instantly the axe in the old man's hand
Began to scream like a hawk; he huddled it against his thigh, saying
　　"Hush, be quiet."

Then he reflects:

　　　　　　　　　　"We and the Russians
Are," he said, "great destroyers—and God will decide the issue. You
　　have perhaps heard some false reports
On the subject of God. He is not dead, and he is not a fable. He is not
　　mocked nor forgotten—
Successfully. God is a lion that comes in the night. God is a hawk
　　gliding among the stars—
If all the stars and the earth, and the living flesh of the night that flows
　　in between them, and whatever is beyond them,
Were that one bird. He has a bloody beak and harsh talons, he
　　pounces and tears—
And where is the German Reich? There also
Will be prodigious America and world-owning Russia. I say that all
　　hopes and empires will die like yours;
Mankind will die; there will be no more fools; wisdom will die; the
　　very stars will die;
One fierce life lasts."[62]

In no other phrase has Robinson Jeffers summed up more point-
edly the intensity of his thought and feeling about the nature of
God. It clinches at the essence of insight, his ineradicable faith
about the ultimate, its indestructible essence. All phenomena are
transient, and man more so than not, but *one fierce life lasts*.

　　　　　　　　　　　　While he spoke, his axe
Barked like a hunting eagle but incessantly; the old man lifted his voice
　　to be heard above it;

The German, stunned by their double clamor, flung up his hands to
    his head and returned away from them
Down the dark silent hill. The gaunt old man on the little gray horse
Gazed after him, saying, "God does not care, why should I care?"[63]

But the encounter with the profane mentality is not so easily
put aside. It has its own contagion, for as an archetype it carries
the full weight and emphasis of modernity, and touched by it our
minds suddenly are drained, leaving the visionary mental pro-
clivity to repeat its processes unvivified by the numen. Suddenly
the old man confronts again the Void as he has come to accept it
in his mind's recesses, but now seen in all the naked emptiness
of his spirit's dearth:

    He felt in his mind the vast boiling globes
Of the innumerable stars redden to a deadly starset; their ancient
    power and glory were darkened,
The serpent flesh of the night that flows in between them was not
    more cold. Nothing was perfectly cold,
Nothing was hot; no flow nor motion; lukewarm equality,
The final desert. The old man shuddered and hid his face and said,
"Well, God has died."[64]

But the emptiness cannot hold. The religious spirit can only mo-
mentarily experience the neutrality of the profane, and then all
the vast numinous reality floods back. The Void lives in the truth
of the divine sufficiency, the one fierce life that lasts.

    He shook like an epileptic and saw the darkness glow
    again. Flash after flash,
And terrible midnight beyond midnight, endless succession, the
    shining towers of the universe
Were and were not; they leaped back and forth like goats
Between existence and annihilation. The old man laughed and said,
"Skin beyond skin, there is always something beyond: it comes in and
    stirs them. I think that poor fellow
Should have let in the mad old serpent infinity, the double zero that
    confounds reckoning,
In his equation."[65]

The Void, the mad serpent of infinity, the double zero. Between
the sacral and secular sides of his mind, the poet, in the narrow
point of his consciousness, affirms the duality but has no doubts

or illusions about where, for him, the consequences lie, or what his obligations are. Sucking in his breath, the first intake of affirmation, the old man exclaims, "Skin beyond skin, Lord! O thou All!" He calls the scientist back, offering him refuge on the grounds that he has chosen "free science" over servility, but the man would not return.

✦

THREE

✦

And After the Fire a Still Small Voice

✦

And, behold, the Lord passed by,
And a great and strong wind rent the mountains,
And brake in pieces the rocks before the Lord;
But the Lord was not in the wind:
And after the wind an earthquake;
But the Lord was not in the earthquake:
And after the earthquake a fire;
But the Lord was not in the fire:
And after the fire a still small voice.

I Kings 19: 11–12

✦

I. THE DIVINE FASCINANS

In the essential speechlessness that mysticism is, poetry finds its voice. Like prayer, it moves forever beyond itself to its own extinction. Then it gives up gladly, relinquishing the substance of itself in what it was created to achieve. This is a feature it shares with physical love. In the storm and rapture of the embrace, love transcends itself by centering itself. The phallus knocking at the womb, like the tongue stuttering in the throat, achieves at climax that expenditure which is its failure, the quintessence of success. I think more than any other form of art, poetry is mysticism's flesh.

I say this because I truly believe if there were no such thing as poetry, mysticism could not be. The God-appetite would be there, as the sex-appetite is there, but their distillation in the imagination is the engendering that makes each evocative. Poetry does for love of God just what it does for love of woman:

> I would lead thee, and bring thee into my mother's house,
> Who would instruct me:
> I would cause thee to drink of spiced wine,
> Of the juice of my pomegranate.
> His left hand should be under my head,
> And his right hand should embrace me.[1]

It is in the order of the imagination, the order of poetry, that the possible exceeds itself, is sanctified in excess.

In the extremes of imagination, the poet and the saint concur. A spiritual writer observes:

The mark of the saint is that he always lives at the limit of his power. There is no one whose life is so close to the spontaneous movements of nature. He seems in a way to surrender to them, to find in them the source and spring of all his action. We may indeed think that he fights against these natural impulses; but it would be more true to say that he directs them all to their final end—to the point at which they bring him perfect satisfaction and fulfillment.[2]

This could be said about poetry, for poetry, like sanctity, is the orchestration of multiple attributes into vast, compelling wholes.

In poetry, the natural goods of the real, tasted and compared, converge upon an acuteness that outstrips them. What is truly whole in the order of nature becomes our glory-hole to the divine. As in bed the great lover, *maestro*, orchestrates the substance of desire and perception: the merging and the tautness; breast, lip, belly, thighs; the clutch of buttocks; the sweep and shudder of convulsive flanks; and the ultimate, toiled enclosure of the grip-of-love, our body's knot of consequence. So does the poet, wrestling in his soul, master into convergence the separate relatedness of concept and savor, fear, equivocation, anxiety consummated in the tang of lust—from these pressings the harmonic, that synthesis, achieves the utterance of the sole resolving chord, beatitude, the pure note.

The mystic speaks. What impels him is his whole incentive, the fascination. Obsessed by enchantment, tantalized by the imperceptible, he yields up his reason to his instinct, and his instinct, liberated, guides his intelligence. Thus he fortifies security in the matchless subsumption beyond securitative needs. Fructification takes him. He grapples God on earth, God in the sea, God in the sky. He smells him out in bed. At the Table of the Lord, he eats divinity, devours God's flesh. He is insatiable because the food that feeds him incites him in his hunger. Hunger is his need, and his need is unstanchable. Reason may balk, but imagination knows no end. Never exhausting the modes of its obsession because love is inexhaustible, like the lover who has never possessed his beloved in all the possessable ways, he relinquishes possession in order to be trapped, in order to be possessed.

Laughing, she eludes him, cool-throated and provocative, disappearing in the dusk. In high school there is always a girl whom every boy desires but none dares touch. "Jesus," one will say, speaking for them all, "I wish she would lose me in the alfalfa and dare me to pull down her pants." She never does. Tongues hanging out, groping in the moonlit nights of the imagination, they search all through the haystacks of the San Joaquin and never corner her. Her disdain is unspeakable.

Robinson Jeffers became a poet when he gave up fantasies and got his teeth into the language of appetite and need, of substance, tangibility, concreteness, in order to masticate from the essence, the perdurable abstract. He became a lover when the poetry that was hollowing his head finally invaded his arms and filled up his being. He became a mystic when his poetry and his love transcended each other into a consummation neither alone was capable of. But that was not the end. In the end it was the mysticism that perfected him in love, the love that perfected him in poetry.

And he must have lost them all more than once through obsession, his appetite, and regained them again through his faith. Many a time his muse must have lured him out into the alfalfa, but like the disdainful girl in the moonlight, she left him with empty arms, leveled with God. He was not worthy of her; he is now not worthy of Him.

Redoubling its energies on its divine food, the soul exceeds itself. Filling the essence of its need in its arms, the imagination over-leaps and goes on. *Fascinans!* The divine obsession. God beyond God beyond God calls to ineffable consummations. All among the haystacks of the summer nights, the Shulamite, Divine Wisdom, enchants the soul. Like an Armenian girl deceiving her mother, she slips out into the darkness, disappears behind the barn, laughing, cool-throated in the dusk, to reappear in the orchard. O son of man, how far will you pursue her, and what will you offer her in the laying down of your life? Or will you dodge and dance away, to boast next morning of pulling shirttails with her, boasting when the fellows jostle before school, pushing and shoving, and waste their substance? What is the worth of your imagination, the price, the *value* you place on your fascination? Brace yourself, O youthful seeker! That woman will demand proof. She who most allures will purge in pain all your braggadocio to elude you at the orchard's end and break your heart. It is the pain she holds in her fingertips that makes her what she is, makes revulsion vie with fascination, and makes fascination triumph. Oh, more crucial than contesting angels, those attributes compete in her, those attributes complete her. When you think of her, when you long to hold her in your arms again and taste on her tongue the seedcake with which she fed and will feed forever, the nerve of your enchantment, do not forget the meaning she leaves you with—the meaning that all she is, whatever she is, is not meant to be enough.

What, then, is the *fascinans*, the divine attraction? Though Otto does not say so, it seems to me to be, in its evocative intangibility, the feminine aspect of God. For if the *tremendum* reveals the masculine element in the divine—the power, the wrath, the thunder, and the awe, what could be called the Yang—then the *mysterium*, which is its counterpart and is the essence of attractiveness, typifies the Yin. Where the Yang side of God drives one back into oneself, freezing like an animal before the manifestation of power, the Yin—of which the "wholly other" is the hidden—the *fascinans* takes one out, expands the psyche and the soul, opens and enlarges. Fused together, they complete the awesome range and potential of the *mysterium tremendum.* "These two qualities, the daunting and the fascinating, now combine in a strange harmony of contrasts, and the resultant dual character of the numinous consciousness, to which the entire religious development bears witness, is at once the strangest and most noteworthy phenomenon in the whole history of religion."[3]

If this be true, it would seem that we have arrived at the apotheosis point of mystical evolution. This fusion of opposed polarities puts what might be called a warp in the affect, making for a certain strain that recalls the occult, the preternatural, the weird, and disturbs the ideality of our presupposition of the sacred: "The demonic-divine object may appear to the mind an object of horror and dread, but at the same time it is no less something that allures with a potent charm, and the creature, who trembles before it, utterly cowed and cast down, has always at the same time the impulse to turn to it, even to make it somehow his own."[4] These words seem particularly appropriate to the situation Jeffers describes in *Roan Stallion*, which we touched on earlier, but now the focus is sharpened:

> Here is solitude, here on the calvary, nothing conscious
> But the possible God and the cropped grass, no witness, no eye but
>   that misformed one, the moon's past fullness.
> Two figures on the shining hill, woman and stallion, she kneeling to
>   him, brokenly adoring,
> He cropping the grass, shifting his hooves, or lifting the long head to
>   gaze over the world,
> Tranquil and powerful. She prayed aloud, "O God, I am not good
>   enough, O fear, O strength, I am draggled."[5]

In this passage, of course, the stallion stands for the Yang side of the divine archetype, the power and the majesty. By situating it on the mountain top, at the center of the cosmos, as it were, all the numinous majesty of the universe seems concretized in the masculine symbol. But when we ask what constitutes the *fascinans*, the Yin, we do not find it in the woman. Despite all his sympathy for her, Jeffers has not invested the numinous in her. Rather, he has evoked it in the surrounding landscape, the natural setting of the earth, redolent with the subsumed radiance that testifies so hauntingly to the divine:

> She stood then,
> Shaking. Enormous films of moonlight
> Trailed down from the height. Space, anxious whiteness, vastness.
> Distant beyond conception the shining ocean
> Lay light like a haze along the ledge and doubtful world's end. Little
> vapors gleaming, and little
> Darknesses on the far chart underfoot symbolized wood and valley;
> but the air was the element, the moon-
> Saturate arcs and spires of the air.[6]

Here is the *fascinans*, the feminine, compellingly beautiful and attractive, the Yin side of God.

But Otto fails to make this distinction. By ignoring the gender equation, he restricts his options to descriptive exposition, leaving untapped the immense resources of the feminine: " 'Mystery' is for him [the worshipper] not merely something to be wondered at but something that entrances him; and besides that in it which bewilders and confounds, he feels a something that captivates and transports him with a strange ravishment, rising often enough to the pitch of dizzy intoxication; it is the Dionysiac-element in the numen."[7]

Indeed it is, but more pertinently it is the feminine standing opposite the attributed objectivity and detachment of the masculine norm, the Apollonian. In order to grasp the broad spectrum of the feminine archetype in Jeffers's work—not only the dithyrambic but also the hidden side in the representation of which Jeffers excels—let us turn first to a poem that may well be his finest, his masterpiece in the short form. It is called "Night."

> The ebb slips from the rock, the sunken
> Tide-rocks lift streaming shoulders
> Out of the slack, the slow west
> Sombering its torch; a ship's light
> Shows faintly, far out,

Over the weight of the prone ocean
On the low cloud.

Over the dark mountain, over the dark pinewood,
Down the long dark valley along the shrunken river,
Returns the splendor without rays, the shining of shadow,
Peace-bringer, the matrix of all shining and quieter of shining.
Where the shore widens on the bay she opens dark wings
And the ocean accepts her glory. O soul worshipful of her
You like the ocean have grave depths where she dwells always,
And the film of waves above that takes the sun takes also
Her, with more love. The sun-lovers have a blond favorite,
A father of lights and noises, wars, weeping and laughter,
Hot labor, lust and delight and the other blemishes. Quietness
Flows from her deeper fountain; and he will die; and she is immortal.

Far off from here the slender
Flocks of the mountain forest
Move among stems like towers
Of the old redwoods to the stream,
No twig crackling; dip shy
Wild muzzles into the mountain water
Among the dark ferns.

O passionately at peace you being secure will pardon
The blasphemies of glowworms, the lamp in my tower, the
        fretfulness
Of cities, the cressets of the planets, the pride of the stars.
This August night in a rift of cloud Antares reddens,
The great one, the ancient torch, a lord among lost children,
The earth's orbit doubled would not girdle his greatness, one fire
Globed, out of grasp of the mind enormous; but to you O Night
What? Not a spark? What flicker of a spark in the faint far glimmer
Of a lost fire dying in the desert, dim coals of a sand-pit the Bedouins
Wandered from at dawn . . . Ah singing prayer to what gulfs tempted
Suddenly are you more lost? To us the near-hand mountain
Be a measure of height, the tide-worn cliff at the sea-gate a measure of
        continuance.

The tide, moving the night's
Vastness with lonely voices,
Turns, the deep dark-shining
Pacific leans on the land,
Feeling his cold strength

To the outmost margins: you Night will resume
The stars in your time.

O passionately at peace when will that tide draw shoreward?
Truly the spouting fountains of light, Antares, Arcturus,
Tire of their flow, they sing one song but they think silence.
The striding winter giant Orion shines, and dreams darkness.
And life, the flicker of men and moths and the wolf on the hill,
Though furious for continuance, passionately feeding, passionately
Remaking itself on its mates, remembers deep inward
The calm mother, the quietness of the womb and the egg,
The primal and the latter silences: dear Night it is memory
Prophesies, prophecy that remembers, the charm of the dark.
And I and my people, we are willing to love the four-score years
Heartily; but as a sailor loves the sea, when the helm is for harbor.

Have men's minds changed,
Or the rock hidden in the deep of the waters of the soul
Broken the surface? A few centuries
Gone by, was none dared not to people
The darkness beyond the stars with harps and habitations.
But now, dear is the truth. Life is grown sweeter and lonelier,
And death is no evil.[8]

Many other contemplative poems of Jeffers fall into place under
this aspect of the Yin, and one of them, "Continent's End," in fact
rivals "Night" for top honors. Also, all the narratives contain pas-
sages of sublime feeling, serving to heal the painful action in the
balm of the transcendent, as we saw in *Roan Stallion*.

Returning to Otto's probing of the numinous as the clue to the
fusion of two polarities, the "daunting" and the "fascinating," as
the core of the religious pursuit, we have just seen the Yin-state
at the full of quiescence. But increase the torque of the Yang, and
the passion surges toward the dithyrambic. In "At the Fall of an
Age," the Myrmidons are lined up to watch the death of Helen,
having followed her from the death of Achilles, so that no other
man may possess her.

Wild swan, splendid-bodied,
Silent at last, silent and proud, fly up the dark.
Clash bronze, beat shields, beauty is new-born.
It is not to be whispered in Argos that Helen died like a woman,
Nor told in Laconia that sickness killed her.

Strike swords, blade on blade, the daughter of God
Hangs like a lamp, high in the dark, quivering and white.
The breasts are thrust forward and the head bows, the fleece of gold
Shakes on the straining shoulders, writhes to the long white thighs.
When God looked down from heaven the mound in the Troad
Swarmed like an anthill, what spears are those?
Power that will pierce your people, God of the living,
The warrior-ants of the anthill, the spears from the dark barrow . . .
                                    . . .
Look under the torches, Oh King, that flare in the wind of night,
Look under the torches.
No Dorians are we; they planted strange seed in Asia who buried
        Achilles,
Power to pierce death, helmeted heads cracking the grass-roots,
Power to be born again.
Come down and behold us Oh King of heaven and Oh hawks of
        Caucasus,
Come down and behold us,
You African lions in the tawny wilderness roar in the storm,
For our master is joined with the beauty he remembered in death, with
        the splendor of the earth,
While the King of Laconia howls like a starved dog
In the rain, in the violet lightnings, in the gaps of night, and we hold
        the gates.[9]

In such passages we see not only how the specific religious ref-
erences—such as "daughter of God," "God of the living," "King
of heaven," and so forth—designate the numen, but more par-
ticularly how the incantatory rhythms, the violence of the im-
agery, and the power and range of the imaginative sweep evince
it directly, give us the "Dionysiac element in the numen."

However, though Jeffers is, as we have seen, the poet *par ex-
cellence* of these more primitive aspects of the *fascinans*, responses
in which the daunting retains a markedly predominant element
of the numenal composite, he is nevertheless no stranger to its
more subtle manifestation. Putting aside the vast cosmic sweep
or the exultant throb of passion expended in which to localize the
numinous, he can take up the quieter moments, validate them as
instances of ineffable quiescence, let the numinous rise mysteri-
ously to possess the poem, and allow the sheer *fascinans* to show
forth virtually untouched by the daunting element.

In "Oh, Lovely Rock," he describes a trip back into the coastal mountains, he and his son and companion making camp on graveled sand up Ventana Creek. While the others sleep, Jeffers rekindles the spent fire and, roused from suspenseful thought, becomes aware of the presence overhead:

> it was the rock wall
> That fascinated my eyes and mind. Nothing strange: light-grey diorite
>   with two or three slanting seams in it,
> Smooth-polished by the endless attrition of slides and floods; no fern
>   nor lichen, pure naked rock . . . as if I were
> Seeing rock for the first time. As if I were seeing through the flame-lit
>   surface into the real and bodily
> And living rock. Nothing strange . . . I cannot
> Tell you how strange: the silent passion, the deep nobility and
>   childlike loveliness: this fate going on
> Outside our fates. It is here in the mountain like a grave smiling child.
>   I shall die, and my boys
> Will live and die, our world will go on through its rapid agonies of
>   change and discovery; this age will die,
> And wolves have howled in the snow around a new Bethlehem: this
>   rock will be here, grave, earnest, not passive: the energies
> That are its atoms will still be bearing the whole mountain above: and
>   I, many packed centuries ago,
> Felt its intense reality with love and wonder, this lonely rock.[10]

Or he can touch just in passing the latent erotic element in this same aspect of the *fascinans*, as when Gudrun exclaims:

> I have come to my love, I have
>   found him. Here is the dignity
> We adored in rocks and waters, the reticent self-contained,
>   self-watchful passion of the gray rock[11]

Thus Jeffers is by no means the single-natured, Yang-minded poet, hostile to the feminine, as some have accused. But for him neither is the Yin, the *fascinans*, a delicate handmaid. Rather, her magic is swift and powerful. She captures with a direct hand and holds the poet, his eyes blinking with tears, throat constricted, mouth open with awe. She is more beautiful than he can ever find words for. If he tries over and over, it is because the grip she has on his heart is relentless. She compels with an awesome attraction. In him she has found not only her voice, the song of her tenderness, but the sudden seizure of her lust.

II. RITUAL PROPITIATION

In the voice of her tenderness and the holy seizure of her lust, the divine Yin compels. Her lust is the pulse of regeneration, the reopening of her womb to the influxing and transformative Ray. In his propitiation the poet partakes of the essence of all ritual, of all liturgy. He redramatizes the epic of creation: impregnation, the conception of new form, the creation of the world. The pulse of lust, pure potentiality, intoxicates him, and he responds. Seizing his stylus, he exacts of the inchoate the authority of mind. He precipitates creation.

Man ritualizes, always, in order to step out of the tyranny of the temporal, which is death, and make life new. Wherever he pauses in order to abolish time, he enacts the original gesture of creation, enters the order of sacrality, which is life. For the duration of his liturgy, time is denied, thrust back; chaos is divided. He forces it to reveal the archetype of transcendence which underlies it. Thus the ecstasy of the poet. In his act of creation, he ritualizes the character of chaos, makes time "real" by holding it at bay. It is in this that he is a priest.

But it is through time that the poet compels reality into the substance of his form. His words, material elements, have all the character of chaos until his act ordains them to permanence. Jeffers, disdaining the claims of temporality, has said, "I can tell lies in prose."[12] And in a sense all prose, being partial and holistically deficient, is deceptive, falsifying the vibration of reality, and hence "tells lies," this statement being no exception. But poetry is that ordering of the temporality of the physical by which time itself is checked, and out of its abeyance the peace of absolute perception is bodied forth. Poetry is the "sacrifice," the creative act, the ritual by which chaos is divided in order to make coherent the underpinnings of reality, the subsistent "other." Every sacrifice immolates a victim, takes a being out of time and ordains it to timelessness, the holy. Thus every sacrifice is a dividing, a rendering into polarity in order to establish the structure of existence. It precedes and culminates in the articulation of form, of meaning. Every propitiation is a rescuing out of temporality. Christ on the cross, the divine Victim, is self-immolated in order to give form to reality, wrest form out of chaos. The poet as sacrificer offers the raw materials of language, creates a separation into opposites, and a synthesis into wholeness. In his act of creation is his act of wholeness, his act of existence.

Therefore it is not surprising to see the poet in his creative deed follow the outlines of the original rituals. Before the purity of the page, the purity of preexistence, poets choreograph the movements of their liturgy. For the religious poet, this purity is the same terrible blankness of the empty page the secular poet stands aghast of, shaken by the omnipresence of his impotence. But for him, the religious poet, that blankness is not so much sterility as it is inchoation, the lightlessness of preexistence which has to be transformed into the white light of the real, "the light around the body." What it needs is a victim to make it divide into opposites. The victim is the Word.

It is the manifestation of the Word by which the undifferentiated character of preexistence is abolished. Once it is uttered, the awful anonymity of silence is shattered. Once it is set down, space becomes dynamic, takes on tension, vivification, opportunity, consequence. The poet creates. He repeats the primal mythic ritual of creation. His utterance and his inscription have established polarity. Phenomena spring into being.

Jeffers, born a poet, became a master in the year 1921, upon the death of his mother. The old matrix passed away. For nine months he had lain in the womb of her body being nurtured into form. For 34 years he had lain in the womb of her psyche, her dream of existence, fashioned by the flux of her imagination and the pulse of her spirit. When she passed away at last, he stepped forth from the caul of her sheltering (she died under Pisces, the sign of his ascendent), stepped out of the ribs of her dismemberment like a living heart seized up from the body of sacrifice, and spoke. The word he spoke was uttered in the secret image of her imagination, the inchoate spirit of the feminine, the pulsing lust of the Yin. The word he spoke was "Tamar"!

Writing her poem was his first efficacious ritual of the spirit. He had gotten sons out of the womb of his bride-mother to build him a memorial of the flesh in the continuity of his name. And he had gotten stones out of the womb of the sea to make him a sacred space, a living tower, against the ravages of time. But always before, his first sacrificial attempts—the creation of poems—had been inefficacious. His materials, his words, had lain damp within the body of her womb, and he could not ignite them. When she died, he stepped forth fully blown, invincible, and uttered the name of the secret, incestuous Yin, whose offering to life he was—"Tamar"!

It is of the essence that the poet's definitive acts always partake of the archetypal, always repeat a paradigmatic model. In this his ancestry is enormously deep—so deep, in fact, that time has no power over it. Through these acts he maintains his poise against the ravages of transition. His being is authenticated in permanence because his primitive instinct has hardly permitted him to emerge from the matrix of eternity. Eliade writes: "This conscious repetition of given paradigmatic gestures reveals an original ontology. The crude product of nature, the objects fashioned by the industry of man, acquire their reality, their identity, only to the extent of their participation in a transcendent reality. The gesture acquires meaning, reality, solely to the extent to which it repeats a primordial act."[13]

Yeats understood this, and so did Rilke. And indeed there are many others of whom its truth became the essence of their contribution. But I think that of them all, Jeffers lived it in a special, uncompromising way; grave, austere, hieratic, unremitting, he refused to compromise his symbols to the urgencies of temporality. He made his concessions, true, but like a desert hermit they were only wrung from him, and they were minimal. He conceded; he did not compromise.

Otto does not treat of ritual as the reconstitution of a paradigmatic creative act, but as a transaction, a means of gaining control over the numen. He is probing the roots of mysticism and sees the liturgical gesture as a means of appropriating the *fascinans*, putting it to the service of man, a kind of magic. His thesis does not have, therefore, the comprehensiveness of Eliade, who, as we

have seen, situates ritual as gesture in a graver and more mean-
ingful context. But we may follow with profit, at least as it applies
to Jeffers, Otto's division of ceremonials into two basic categories:
"On the one hand the 'magical' identification of the self with the
numen proceeds by means of various transactions at once mag-
ical and devotional in character—by formula, ordination, adjur-
ation, consecration, exorcism, etc. On the other hand are the
'shamanistic' ways of procedure, possession, indwelling, self-
fulfillment in exaltation and ecstasy."[14] Certainly of these two
ways, the magical and the shamanistic, the latter is of far more
interest to Jeffers, who more than once credits ritual transactional
attempts with a certain efficacy. In accommodating him to Otto,
let us follow him through these, not so much to see whether the
practices he depicts are accurate reconstitutions of occult meth-
ods, but to sense in his use of them that quality corresponding to
the part of the soul from which they originated, to use them as
gauges of his authentic religious disposition. If the mood be true,
we shall not pause to inquire whether or not he has accurately
depicted an existent ritual method.

As a beginning, let us take the poem "Come, Little Birds." Here
Jeffers narrates a vivid episode, presumably autobiographical,
wherein contact with the world beyond is secured through a
primitive sacrificial liturgy.

> The old woman brought us to a tongue of grassed land
>   under the stream-bank;
> One of her boys gathered dry sticks for a fire, the other cleared and
>   repaired a short shallow trench
> That scored the earth there; then they heaped up the sticks and made
>   yellow flame, about ten feet from the trench
> On the north side, right against the water; the woman sat opposite the
>   fire and facing it, gazing northward,
> Her back against a big stone.   She closed her eyes and hummed
>   tuneless music, nodding her vulturine head
> To the dull rhythm; through which one heard the fire snoring and the
>   river flowing, and the surf on the shore
> Over the hill. After some time she widened her eyes, and their sight
>   was rolled up
> Under her forehead. I saw the firelight

Flicker on the blank whites; she raised her arms and cried out
In a loud voice. Instantly her two boys went up and fetched the black
    calf though he plunged and struggled.
They tied his hind feet with a tight knot, and passed the bight of the
    rope over a sycamore bough
That hung above the stream and the head of the trench; they tugged
    his hind feet up to it, so that he fell
On the knees of his forelegs over the trench-head. Then one of the two
    young men sheared the calf's throat
With a sharp knife, holding him by one ear, the other by an ear and
    the nostrils, and the blood spouted
Into the furrow. The woman, her body twitching convulsively. "Come,
    little birds."
She screamed through her tightened throat like a strangling person,
"Put on the life, here is the blood, come, you gray birds."[15]

Jeffers uses a similar technique in "The Bowl of Blood," en-
abling Hitler to converse with certain spirits of the past in an at-
tempt to determine the course of his strategy. Here the blood is
swine's blood, perhaps a symbolic difference; yet the basic tech-
nique is the same. The medium inhales the fumes of blood in or-
der to evoke the dead. All primitives held that blood is the prin-
ciple of life, and for many its use drew the dead to it. Odysseus
in Avernus is the classic instance.
    At a more crucial level, Jeffers himself ritualizes, a direct cere-
monial utilization toward a method in poetic composition. In
"Apology for Bad Dreams," stunned by the overwhelming beauty
of the coast, he invokes propitiation against its excessiveness:

This coast crying out for tragedy like all beautiful places: and like the
    passionate spirit of humanity
Pain for its bread: God's, many victims', the painful deaths, the
    horrible transfigurements: I said in my heart,
"Better invent than suffer: imagine victims
Lest your own flesh be chosen the agonist, or you
Martyr some creature to the beauty of the place." And I said,
"Burn sacrifices once a year to magic
Horror away from the house, this little house here
You have built over the ocean with your own hands
Beside the standing boulders: for what are we,
The beast that walks upright, with speaking lips
And little hair, to think we should always be fed,

Sheltered, intact, and self-controlled? We sooner more liable
Than the other animals. Pain and terror, the insanities of desire; not
    accidents but essential,
And crowd up from the core:" I imagined victims for those wolves, I
    made them phantoms to follow,
They have hunted the phantoms and missed the house.[16]

One of his most beautiful lyrics is built around this same archetypal need to ritualize, to achieve identification with the numen by means of a ritual transaction. In "To the Rock That Will Be a Cornerstone of the House," he brings the ancient ingredients of ruddy wine and white milk and honey for an invocational offering:

I did not dream the taste of wine could bind with granite,
Nor honey and milk please you; but sweetly
They mingle down the storm-worn cracks among the mosses,
Interpenetrating the silent
Wing-prints of ancient weathers long at peace, and the older
Scars of primal fire, and the stone
Endurance that is waiting millions of years to carry
A corner of the house, this also destined.
Lend me the stone strength of the past and I will lend you
The wings of the future, for I have them.
How dear you will be to me when I too grow old, old comrade.[17]

In *Tamar*, also, Jeffers ritualizes during intervals between the nodes of action, in order to gain a certain distance and to establish the dimension of the divine in a ritualistic apostrophe:

O swiftness of the swallow and strength
Of the stone shore, brave beauty of falcons,
Beauty of the blue heron that flies
Opposite the color of evening
From the Carmel River's reed-grown mouth
To her nest in the deep wood of the deer
Cliffs of peninsular granite engirdle,
O beauty of the fountains of the sun
I pray you enter a little chamber,
I have given you bodies, I have made you puppets,
I have made idols for God to enter
And tiny cells to hold your honey.
I have given you a dotard and an idiot,

An old woman puffed with vanity, youth but botched with incest,
O blower of music through the crooked bugles,
You that make signs of sins and choose the lame for angels,
Enter and possess. Being light you have chosen the dark lamps,
A hawk the sluggish bodies: therefore God you chose
Me; and therefore I have made you idols like these idols
To enter and possess.[18]

And in a similar way in *The Women at Point Sur*, he pauses to invoke the overmastering power upon the work of his hands, seeking to establish for it the gravity and epic scale his vision demands:

Here were new idols again to praise him;
I made them alive; but when they looked up at the face before they
    had seen it they were drunken and fell down.
I have seen and not fallen, I am stronger than the idols,
But my tongue is stone how could I speak him? My blood in my veins
    is seawater how could it catch fire?
The rock shining dark rays and the rounded
Crystal the ocean his beam of blackness and silence
Edged with azure, bordered with voices;
The moon her brittle tranquillity; the giant phantoms, the fountains of
    light, the seed of the sky,
Their plaintive splendors whistling to each other:
There is nothing but shines though it shine darkness; nothing but
    answers;
                              . . .
                    they are woven in the nerve-warp.
One people, the stars and the people, one structure; the voids between
    stars, the voids between atoms, and the vacancy
In the atom in the rings of the spinning demons,
Are full of that weaving; one emptiness, one presence: who had
    watched all his splendor
Had known but a little: all his night, but a little.
I made glass puppets to speak of him, they splintered in my hand and
    have cut me, they are heavy with my blood.
But the jewel-eyed herons have never beheld him
Nor heard; nor the tall owl with cat's ears, the bittern in the willows,
    the squid in the rock in the silence of the ocean,
The vulture that broods in the pitch of the blue
And sees the earth globed, her edges dripping into rainbow twilights:
    eyed hungers, blind fragments: I sometime

Shall fashion images great enough to face him
A moment and speak while they die. These here have gone mad: but
  stammer the tragedy you crackled vessels.[19]

Thus Jeffers, priest of the word, victimizes the imagination in order to purge the proud flesh of man's primordial wound. Stooping over the pit of potentiality, he plucks from chaos the figures of redemption. These emerge bleeding with inchoation, with none to know who or what till the liturgy is fulfilled. Then, struck with strangeness, the aura of their nascence still burning about them, they seize life and sing. Their voices, pure tonalities, only hauntingly translate into speech. When the liturgy is completed and they disappear into time, he rouses from birth-trance and, peering about him, discovers their words in his book.

III. THE VOICE OF THE SHAMAN

"All true wisdom," said the Eskimo shaman Igjugaruk to Rasmussen, the Danish explorer, "is found far from men, out in the great solitude, and it can be acquired only through suffering. Privations and sufferings are the only things that can open a man's mind to that which is hidden from others."[20] Silence, suffering, and solitude, the holy trinity that compels the shaman to his calling, also keep him there. In his techniques of ecstasy, he returns to the primordial wound and revives his vocation by recourse to interior pain. He seeks isolation because the relativity of life becomes excruciatingly distractive, and the "great solitude," the uncrossable ice floe of his interior landscape, enables him to concentrate on the essentiality of his pain, which is his obsession.

Twirling his rattle like a spinning maple seed descending in the air, the shaman croons his melody of sustenance and participation. He crouches over his little drum and beats up rhythms that will sustain him in his flight. Huddled over his fire, he feels about him the vast Arctic night, the wind over the steppes like a razor-honed harpoon. The emptiness seems like something preternaturally alive, a living, threatening presence. He feels within himself the suck downward into the black descent that is yet the flight that transforms it all. In his ordeal of faith, he steels the marrow of his bones, the fiber of his nerves, for the supreme effort. Only by surpassing himself can he redeem the race that sends him into death.

Spiraling down to it, impelled by his ritual drum and rattle, as a grebe dives beneath the surface of the water, the shaman plunges into the underblows of tribal life to seek the dying spirit that had drowned without him. When he finds it, he revives it by projecting that spirit forth in a unique form, a form collective as a model but personal to the ineluctable impress of his anguish. Because the dross of impersonality is quickened in the fire of personal transcendence, his act is supremely efficacious. In this he prefigures the poet.

For as the shaman, the poet, too, descends down the torrents of his self to find the spirit that languishes in death. There the elements of consciousness lie torn and sundered, split by the contrarieties of existence, the flaws that only an heroic spiritual victory can unify. Both differ from the mere conjurer in that the repetition of the salvific model itself does not suffice. Each must distinguish the object of his obsession by the uniqueness of his suffering; each must body it forth in a truly paradigmatic instance that is yet endowed with uniqueness by the personal intensity he brings to it. The famous bison of the Altamira caves, paintings which prefigure so intensely some of the most salient compounds of modern art, are distinguished not so much by the representations of the animal as a paradigmatic model, but by the articulation of a spiritual shape recreated through the interior travail of terror or awe into transcendent, and hence efficacious, form. Thus the poet shamanizes, not by the incorporation of archaic or mythological or religious elements into his verse, but by the singling intensity in which he engages his obsession in his own creative act.

The poet also follows the shaman in his reliance upon the state of trance to perform his act of efficacious creativity. In trance, in ecstasy, the shaman frees himself from the imbalance of the here-and-now in order to enter into the state of dynamic equilibrium. His sacred drum and rattle maintain the pulsation of eternity, the reordering of time to embrace and make available the quality of pure duration. For the poet, too, everything depends upon the quality and prolongation of the creative trance, within which he is enabled to engage his demon, his obsession. As long as this

trance subsists, he possesses authority over the images of his un-
conscious; but with the subsidence of the trance, his powers
wane. Yet this trance is not merely individual: it is collective as
well. Out in the "great solitude," the shaman wrestles with the
tribal images his people have impounded within him. And hence
in the principled solitude of his self-imposed condition of "cun-
ning, silence, and exile," the modern poet goes forth to "forge in
the smithy of his soul the uncreated conscience of his race."[21] This
smithy is nothing but the volcanic heart, a smoldering in the guts,
the viscera of his people, the shaman's realm.

For every tribal or collective entity relies upon some practitio-
ner or other to relieve it of the impasse of its temporality: priest
or savant, philosopher or medicine man, preacher or poet. But
according to Andreas Lommel, there is a profound distinction,
even at the primitive level, between the mere functionary and the
efficacious practitioner. "The psychological difference between
medicine man and shaman lies in the totally different evolution
which leads each of them to his calling, the totally different per-
sonality structure and inner attitude to the community."[22] It be-
comes apparent that the shaman emerges as that type of man
whose capacity to help the world is utterly dependent on his ca-
pacity to help himself. As the archetypal man, his probe into self-
knowledge is the probe into universality.

To shamanize means to render the "spirits" subservient to oneself. The
spirits are inner images. Ideas of a personal or collective kind that have
taken on form, images from the mythology of the tribe, of the group,
very old traditional ideas, the whole complex of beliefs belonging to the
so-called "animal level."

The shaman gives these images shape by portraying them and iden-
tifying himself with them, recognizing and using them as real forces, in-
terpreting them artistically. Shamanizing seems to be that psychic tech-
nique by means of which one can subordinate "the spirits" to oneself,
that is to say, bring order into one's own chaotic psyche and gain control
of the power of one's own unconscious imagery. This seems to be pos-
sible in an ever-repeated state of trance.[23]

Thus it would seem that for both shaman and poet, his calling
depends upon his relation to his pain, and if he should become
cured, that is, rendered insensible to his obsession, his shaman-
izing will cease. Freudian psychoanalysts frequently instruct art-

ists who seek clarification that to be successfully analyzed might well mean the end of artistic productivity. There is a shaman's song from the Eskimo:

> I saw with my eyes
> Heard with my ears,
> What others could not
> See or hear when
>
> I was only twenty,
> For I was ill. Nine
> Years I fought myself
> And then became
>
> A shaman. Recovered
> From my cliff of death
> I still slip back
> Unless I can be shaman.[24]

For the shaman maintains interior stability in the face of his obsession only by shamanizing. It is his ever-recurrent recourse to trance through the techniques of ecstasy that keeps him in personal equilibrium. And the collective equilibrium depends upon his recurrent recourse to trance—because the shaman is the tribal link to the sources of calm. His calm after trance becomes the polarity, the center of tribal equilibrium. The calmness of the shaman in the tribal midst is the witness of cosmic unity, the assurance that "all's right with the world." Thus the shaman is essential to the tribal life. As Lommel declares: "A group of aborigines might be compared to a termite state. A termite state is an organism whose limbs are the individual insects. The life of such a termite state ceases if the queen is removed. Similarly life is extinguished among the aborigines if they lose their shaman or he loses his powers."[25] And even today it is said that when a nation loses its poets, it loses its soul.

Jeffers's links to shamanhood can be approached from several perspectives. For instance, it is known that shamanism on the American continent has a particularly close relationship with the world of animals. "The call by an animal spirit is of particularly frequent occurrence in America, the more so as the sense of solidarity between man and animal is there so strong that the two are thought to be linked by a common ancestor. Thus it is often the animal ancestor who calls upon the novice to become a sha-man."[26] Whatever this vibration is that obtains on the Western continent, it is certain that Jeffers witnesses to it in a special way, unique among modern writers. In such poems as "Hurt Hawks," it becomes omnipresent, and the unforgettable eagle's death in *Cawdor* is surely a symbolic depiction of Jeffers's own desired death-flight. The presence of the horse in *Roan Stallion* comes forcefully to mind, and who can forget that other episode in *Cawdor* where Fera assumes the panther skin and draws to herself the bullet of Hood?

In his last, posthumous volume, Jeffers's poem "Vulture" takes the matter to the end. Prone on a hilltop, the poet-speaker becomes aware that a turkey vulture is circling him, hoping he is dead:

> But how beautiful he looked,
> gliding down
> On those great sails; how beautiful he looked, veering away in the
> sea-light over the precipice. I tell you solemnly
> That I was sorry to have disappointed him. To be eaten by that beak
> and become part of him, to share those wings and those eyes—
> What a sublime end of one's body, what an enskyment; what a life
> after death.[27]

This accessibility to the animal presence as a totemistic experience extends down to vegetation and stone. For Jeffers, rocks are almost as alive as hawks. Jeffers's friend, the Irish visionary Ella Young, who claimed to be able to converse with trees and mountains, suggested the same ability for Jeffers. In her book *Flowering Dusk*, she confirmed the shamanistic animism of the American continental presence: "This country is a lioness, a tawny, alert, passionate, austere, beautiful, splendid—perhaps terrible—thing."[28]

Rudolf Otto, in his reference to the shamanistic element in religious experience, does not specify the matter as closely as does Lommel, whose approach we have so far followed. As a term, he uses it simply as counter to the opposite category of the ritualistic; but the element he introduces under its heading he sees as basic. For Lommel shamanism was the beginning of art; for Otto the same phenomenon denotes the beginning of religious life itself. "Possession, indwelling, and self-fulfillment in exaltation and ecstasy, are, in this point of view, the beginning of a whole new approach to the religious dimension." Nor is this to be wondered at, for Otto tells us that whereas:

> All these have, indeed, their starting points simply in magic, and their attention at first was certainly simply to appropriate the prodigious force of the numen for the natural ends of man . . . the process does not rest there. Possession of and by the numen becomes an end in itself; it begins to be sought for its own sake; and the wildest and most artificial methods of asceticism are put into practice to attain it. In a word, the *vita religiosa* begins; and to remain in these strange and bizarre states of numinous possession becomes a good in itself, even a way of salvation, wholly different from the profane goods pursued by means of magic.[29]

Now Jeffers, in his depictions of shamanistic personalities, does not validate their subjective states to the degree that sacral cultures traditionally have done; in fact, he confines their representations to half-wits, drunkards, the insane, and the distraught, thereby keeping his finger on the nerve of our pervasive skepticism. But that these marginal and borderline mentalities enter in fact into a realm of meaning more inclusive than the normative consciousness of his protagonists, he does not question. And occasionally in shorter poems, he even takes an incident from his own life to teach the same lesson, as with the mad sculptor in "An Artist," or the self-induced stigmatist in "A Redeemer." In them he leaves no doubt that, despite his removal from such phenomena, he sees them as actually constituting a perspective superior to the quotidian reality by which he, as a secular man, chooses to live. But above and beyond the aesthetic prudence that keeps him accommodated to the attitudes of his readers, there is evidence that Jeffers himself had personal experience of the visionary states that he reproduces in his characters. His remarkable consonance with the contours of prophetic vision seems too authentic to be merely literary. To take an instance, Tamar's visionary experience in recovering from the shock of miscarriage:

> About the hour of sundown
> Tamar was dreaming trivially—an axman chopping down a tree and
>   field-mice scampering
> Out of the roots—when suddenly like a shift of wind the dream
> Changed and grew awful, she watched dark horsemen coming out of
>   the south, squadrons of hurrying horsemen

Between the hills and the dark sea, helmeted like the soldiers of the
    war in France,
Carrying torches. When they passed Mal Paso Creek the columns
Veered, one of the riders said, "Here it began," but another answered,
    "No. Before the granite
Was bedded to build the world on." So they formed and galloped
    north again, hurrying squadrons,
And Tamar thought, "When they come to the Carmel River then it will
    happen. They have passed Mal Paso."[30]

Compare this with the first vision of Black Elk, a Sioux shaman:

It was when I was five years old that my grandfather made me a bow and
some arrows. The grass was young and I was on horseback. A thunder-
storm was coming from where the sun goes down, and just as I was rid-
ing into the woods along a creek, there was a kingbird sitting on a limb.
This was not a dream, it happened. And I was going to shoot at the king-
bird with the bow my Grandfather made, when the bird spoke and said:
"The clouds all over are one sided." Perhaps it meant that all the clouds
were looking at me. And then it said: "Listen! A voice is calling you!"
Then I looked up at the clouds, and two men were coming there, head-
first like arrows coming down; and as they came, they sang a sacred song
and the thunder was like drumming. I will sing it for you. The song and
the drumming were like this:

> Behold, a sacred voice is calling you;
> All over the sky a sacred voice is calling.

I sat there gazing at them, and they were coming from the place where
the giant lives (north). But when they were very close to me, they
wheeled about toward where the sun goes down and suddenly they
were geese. Then they were gone, and the rain came with a big wind and
a roaring.[31]

Note the strange atmosphere, the oblique perspective, the sur-
real imagery, the singsong trancelike rhythms. The authentic
quality of the preternatural pervades both accounts.
    Of the various marginal mentalities in Jeffers's poems who ap-
proximate the shamanistic function, undoubtedly the most in-
teresting is the Mexican mystic Vasquez:

This man was that Onorio Vasquez
Who used to live on Palo Corona mountain
With his father and his six brothers, but now they lived
Up Mill Creek Canyon beside the abandoned lime-kiln
On land that was not their own. For yearly on this coast

Taxes increase, land grows harder to hold,
Poor people must move their places. Onorio had wealth
Of visions, but those are not coinable. A power in his mind
Was more than equal to the life he was born to,
But fear, or narrowing fortune, had kept it shut
From a larger life; the power wasted itself
In making purposeless visions, himself perceived them
To have no meaning relative to any known thing: but always
They made him different from his brothers; they gave him
A kind of freedom; they were the jewels and value of his life.
So that when once, at a critical time, they failed
And were not seen for a year, he'd hungered to die.
That was nine years ago; his mind was now quieter,
But still it found all its value in visions.
Between them, he hired out his hands to the coast farms,
Or delved the garden at home.[32]

Here, clearly, without recourse to anthropological evidence, Jeffers reconceives the essentiality of shamanizing to the visionary mentality.

As for Onorio, time and time again Jeffers introduces him, freely employing his psychological bias to open dimensions of consciousness that verge on incoherence but nevertheless reveal the sinew of truth in the motion of events. His great vision in *The Loving Shepherdess*, a narrative from which the quotation above is also taken, may serve as example for many he is granted throughout Jeffers's work. Clare Walker, the wandering shepherdess, in telling Onorio her life story, has confessed that she is pregnant, that doctors have warned her an imperfect pelvic bone structure renders her incapable of surviving childbirth. As she sleeps by the campfire, Onorio broods on her predicament. The incident is given in its entirety because no better example exists of Jeffers's shamanist genius. Notice his masterful handling of interior monologue, his innate facility with the contour of vision. Onorio's perception of cosmic relationships is quite consistent with the findings of mysticism, the history of which contains many instances of archaic mentalities elevated in trance to astonishing sophistication:

Vasquez crouched by the fire
And felt one of those revelations that were in his own regard the
     jewels and value of his life

Approach and begin. First passed—as always
Since Barclay was gone, whom he had taken for incarnate God—
　　ancestral forms against the white cloud,
The high dark heads of Indian migrations, going south along the
　　coast, drawn down from the hungry straits and from Asia,
The heads like worn coins and the high shoulders,
The brown-lipped patient mouths below vulture beaks, and burnished
　　fall of black hair over slant foreheads,
Going up to the Mayan and the Aztec mountains, and sowing the
　　coast. They swept the way and the cloud cleared,
The vision would come: came instead a strong pause.
　　　　　　　　　　　　　　　　　A part of his mind
Wished to remember what the rest had forgotten,
And groping for it in the dark withstood the prepared
Pageant of dreams. He'd read in his curious boyhood
Of the child the mother is found incapable of bearing
Cut from the mother's belly. Both live: the wound
Heals: it was called the Caesarean section. But he, fearing
Whatever thought might threaten to infringe his careful
Chastity of mind, had quickly canceled the memory;
That now sought a new birth; it might save Clare
If he could think of it.
　　　　　　　That revived part
Made itself into the vision, all to no purpose,
His precious dreams were never to the point of life.
Only the imperial name, and the world's
Two-thousand-year and ten-thousand-miles-traveled
Caesarean memory appeared. He imagined at first that the voice
Cried "Ave Maria," but it cried "Ave Caesar."[33]

How curious and potent the juxtaposition of the masculine and
feminine polarities, at point of issue in the mind of the visionary,
and the intrusion in triumph of the secular masculine over the
religious feminine one.

　　　　　　　He saw the firelight-gilded
Timbers of the bridge above; and one of the ewes lifted her head in the
　　light beside Clare sleeping;
The smoke gathered its cloud into a floating globe and these were
　　forgotten. On the globe of the earth
The aquiline-headed Roman, who summed in his one person the
　　powers and ordered science of humanity,
Stood and possessed his orb of empire, and looked at the stars. Then
　　the voice cried

"The pride of the earth."

                           But Vasquez laughed aloud, for the earth was
    a grain of dust circling the fire,
And the fire itself but a spark, among innumerable sparks. The swarm
    of the points of light drifting
No path down darkness merged its pin-prick eyelets into one misty
    glimmer, a millstone in shape,
A coin in shape, a mere coin, a flipped luckpenny: but again Vasquez
Laughed out, for who was the spendthrift sowed them all over the sky,
    indistinguishable innumerable
Fish-scales of light? They drew together as they drifted away no path
    down the wild darkness; he saw
The webs of their rays made them one tissue, their rays that were their
    very substance and power filled wholly
The space they were in, so that each one touched all, there was no
    division between them, no emptiness, and each
Changed substance with all the others and became the others. It was
    dreadful to see
No space between them, no cave of peace nor no night of quietness,
    no blind spot nor no deaf heart, but the tides
Of power and substance flood every cranny; no annihilation, no
    escape but change: it must endure itself
Forever. It has the strength to endure itself. We others, being faintly
    made of the dust of a grain of dust
Have been permitted to fool our patience asleep by inventing death. A
    poor comfort, he thought,
Yet better than none, the imaginary cavern, how we all come
    clamoring
To the gates of our great invention after few years.
Though a cheat, it works.[34]

    This poem was published in 1929 and written a year earlier. Only five years had elapsed since improved telescopes had revealed the existence of galaxies beyond our own. But as shaman to the race, Jeffers had grasped the mystical implications of the scientific breakthrough and established the impact of its relevance on the soul of man.

                  The speckled tissue of universes
Drew into one formed and rounded light, and Vasquez
Worshiped the one light. One eye . . . what, an eye?
A dark mountain with an eye in its cliff? A coal-black stallion
Eyed with one burning eye in the mid brow?

Night has an eye. The poor little vision-seer
Groaned, that he never had wit to understand visions.
See all and know nothing. The eye that makes its own light
And sees nothing but itself. "I am seeing Barclay again,"
He marveled, as who should say "I am seeing God:
But what is God?" He continued gazing,
And beads of sweat spilled from his forehead into the fire-edge
Ashes. He saw at last, neither the eyed mountain
Nor the stallion, nor Barclay, but his own eye
In the darkness of his own face.

                     The circuit was closed:
"I can endure all things," he thought, "forever. I am he
Whom I have sought."[35]

It is a masterpiece of visionary intuition. However disappointing
the unconvincingly motivated protagonist Clare Walker is as the
loving shepherdess, this vision of Onorio Vasquez will endure as
one of the pinnacles of Jeffers's achievement. And when we re-
flect that the catalyst was the psychic ambiguity between the
words "Caesar" and "caesarean," we are given a profound in-
sight into the sources of poetic art.

The same sense of historical relevance subsumed in the cosmic
sweep was caught earlier by Jeffers in *The Tower Beyond Tragedy*,
the first poem after *Tamar* in which the implications of the con-
sequence of vision were extended to the historical dimension.
Cassandra, the Trojan prophetess, is accorded one of Jeffers's
most somber and epochal prophecies, declaring that the years

Are not few of captivity: how many have I stood here
Among the great stones, while the Queen's people
Go in and out of the gate, wearing light linen
For summer and the wet spoils of wild beasts
In the season of storms: and the stars have changed, I have watched
The grievous and unprayed-to constellations
Pile steaming spring and patient autumn
Over the enduring walls: but you over the walls of the world,
Over the unquieted centuries, over the darkness-hearted
Millenniums wailing thinly to be born, O vulture-pinioned
Try into the dark,
Watch the north spawn white bodies and red-gold hair,
Race after race of beastlike warriors; and the cities
Burn, and the cities build, and new lands be uncovered

In the way of the sun to his setting . . . go on farther, what profit
In the wars and the toils? but I say
Where are prosperous people my enemies are, as you pass them O my
     spirit
Curse Athens for the joy and the marble, curse Corinth
For the wine and the purple, and Syracuse
For the gold and the ships; but Rome, Rome,
With many destructions for the corn and the laws and the javelins, the
     insolence, the threefold
Abominable power; pass the humble
And the lordships of darkness, but far down
Smite Spain for the blood on the sunset gold, curse France
For the fields abounding and the running rivers, the lights in the cities,
     the laughter, curse England
For the meat on the tables and the terrible gray ships, for old laws, far
     dominions, there remains
A mightier to be cursed and a higher for malediction
When America has eaten Europe and takes tribute of Asia, when the
     ends of the world grow aware of each other
And are dogs in one kennel, they will tear
The master of the hunt with the mouths of the pack: new fallings, new
     risings[36]

   It is always these people of marginal consciousness, borderline
mentalities hinged between light and darkness, who serve for his
shamanistic interests, his strategic need to drive the normative
mental processes down into some degree of creature conscious-
ness, mitigating the collective hubris, until the attitude of uni-
versal self-exaltation is overcome and dispelled. Barclay himself,
verging on insanity, a minister who freed himself from taboo by
the rape of his daughter, becomes master shaman to mankind.
Once again Jeffers reveals his virtuosity in the contour of vision,
as this excerpt from the torrential narrative reveals:

                         He half slept, and April
Went by in a dream, the region and the blood of deflowerment
Bright through her torn clothing; she smiled with wise eyelids.
Then Barclay felt the torpor drop off like a cloak,
Like a cloud split with lightning . . . certainly this cloud
Has lightning in it, he felt it tingle at the hair roots,
And strain, the strain in the air . . . and he said, "Oh Lord God
Why have you deceived me? Why turned me to these?

To be your gull and love them, I will not be your fool
And take their part against you and their part in destruction, they have
    had their Jesus,
Me also to be hanged on Caucasus?"
                     The region people
Were present in him, his mind contained them, and the others,
Innumerable, covering the earth, cities and fields of humanity, the
    Americas, Asia, the ravenous
Billion of little hungers, the choked obscene desires, the microscopic
    terrors and pities,
All present in that intolerable symbol his daughter
With the bare bleeding wound in her.
                     "These? Against the stars? To
    what end?
For either the ice will come back and bury them, or the earth-crust
    open and fire consume them,
Or much more likely they will have died of slow-rotting age
Millions of years before."[37]

Such potent instances in no wise exhaust the occasions of nu-
minous possession that Jeffers uses to jolt us out of our meretri-
cious complacence and prepare us for vision. Aunt Stella in *Ta-
mar*, the ghost of Gudrun in "At the Birth of an Age," the Maskers
in *The Bowl of Blood*, even Drunken Charlie, who, in the poem by
that name, becomes a shaman—all illustrate enlightenment
through radically displaced states of consciousness. And not in-
frequently Jeffers himself steps out of his role of narrator to as-
sume the prophetic mantle, as when he sees Clare Walker, his
painful shepherdess, etched against the span of history:

           Unhappy shepherdess,
Numbed feet and hands and the face
Turbid with fever:
You love, and that is no unhappy fate.
Not one person but all, does it warm your winter?
Walking with numbed and cut feet
Along the last ridge of migration
On the last coast above the not-to-be-colonized
Ocean, across the streams of the people
Drawing a faint pilgrimage
As if you were drawing a line at the end of the world
Under the columns of ancestral figures:
So many generations in Asia,

So many in Europe, so many in America:
To sum the whole.[38]

Thus, too, in *Such Counsels You Gave to Me*, after Howren falls
poisoned by wife and son, his whole organism convulsed in the
stupendous image of a city-state disintegrating in factional revolt,
Jeffers breaks continuity to chant in an apostrophe to the earth:

> Oh rich
> Clean turbulent wind arching the house-roof,
> Roaring in the creekside redwoods, tearing the mountain oaks: you
> 　　living mountains,
> Palo Corona and the ancient forest, Mount Carmel, Pico Blanco,
> 　　Ventanas, high heads
> With clear snow heavy to-night, and you sea-wall ridges and the
> 　　streaming waters, tall granite rocks
> Burly-shouldered standing watchful in pastures:
> I never imagined that you can pity humanity;
> You ought to pity us, perverse by nature, you are the blessed ones.
> I know that you neither hear nor care, but your presence helps,
> One endures extreme evil more nobly in your presence.
> You are sane and stone; humanity is crafty and cruel and mad.
> As for these two: heal this boy's wounds and this woman's hatred:
> Their souls are worse distorted than their dead man's body:
> Or offer them quickly to the eyeless night
> That waits for souls.[39]

Here race-naughting, as we saw it earlier, combined with an
element we have yet to consider, salvific appeal, is subsumed by
a "self-fulfillment in exaltation and ecstasy" that is the shaman-
istic mode. Whatever the charismatic opportunity it provides
when invested in a dramatic character, its function for the poet
himself is to endow him with a powerful and implicit certitude,
an awesome sense of authority.

Otto writes:

Widely various as these states are in themselves, yet they have this ele-
ment in common, that in them the *mysterium* is experienced in its essen-
tial, positive, and specific character, as something that bestows upon
man a beatitude beyond compare, but one whose real nature he can nei-
ther proclaim in speech nor conceive in thought, but may know only by
direct and living experience. It is a bliss that embraces all those blessings
that are indicated or suggested in positive fashion by any "doctrine of

salvation," and it quickens all of them through and through; but these do not exhaust it. Rather by its all-pervasive, penetrating glow it makes of these very blessings more than the intellect can conceive of them or affirm of them. It gives the peace that passes understanding, and of which the tongue can only stammer brokenly. Only from afar, by metaphors and analogies, do we come to apprehend what it is in itself, and even so our notion is but inadequate and confused.[40]

Moreover, in his discussion of these states of mystical transport, Otto notices that often the negative utterly suffices to carry what no positive specification could reach:

"Eye hath not seen, or ear heard, neither have entered into the heart of man, the things which God hath prepared for them that love him." Who does not feel the exalted sound of these words and the "Dionysiac" element of transport and fervor in them? It is instructive that in such phrases as these, in which consciousness would fain put its highest consummation into words, "all images fall away" and the mind turns from them to grasp expression that is purely negative.[41]

Jeffers, too, on occasion has had recourse to the negative to register this effect of the unspeakableness of what he wishes to denote. Probably the best instance is found in "Not Our Good Luck," from the *Roan Stallion* volume:

That he touched you is no wonder, that you slid from his hand
Is an old known tale to our foreland cypresses, no news to the Lobos
    granite, no marvel
To Point Pinos Light and the beacon at Point Sur.
But here is the marvel, he is nowhere not present, his beauty, it is
    burning in the midland villages
And tortures men's eyes in the alleys of cities.[42]

Other possible citations might be instanced such as this from "Night":

A few centuries
Gone by, was none dared not to people
The darkness beyond the stars with harps and habitations.
But now, dear is the truth. Life is grown sweeter and lonelier
And death is no evil.[43]

Or the following from *The Tower Beyond Tragedy*:

how can I express the excellence I have found, that has
no color but clearness;

No honey but ecstasy; nothing wrought nor remembered; no
    undertone nor silver second murmur
That rings in love's voice, I and my loved are one; no desire but
    fulfilled; no passion but peace,
The pure flame and the white, fierier than any passion; no time but
    spheral eternity[44]

This from *Roan Stallion*:

            The atom bounds-breaking,
Nucleus to sun, electrons to planets, with recognition
Not praying, self-equaling, the whole to the whole, the microcosm
Not entering nor accepting entrance, more equally, more utterly, more
    incredibly conjugate
With the other extreme and greatness; passionately perceptive of
    identity[45]

Or this from *The Loving Shepherdess*:

    It was dreadful to see
No space between them, no cave of peace nor no night of quietness,
    no blind spot nor no deaf heart, but the tides
Of power and substance flood every cranny; no annihilation, no
    escape but change: it must endure itself
Forever.[46]

It is as if the voice of the shaman, glutted on Being appre-
hended, stammers "No!" in denial but succeeds only in shouting
"Yes!" in thunder.

The poet, then, emerges as a greater shaman than any of his
creations. Be they never so convincingly delineated in their states
of visionary rapture, they are but an approximation of the ele-
ment which he himself embodies. Descending in trance to the sa-
cred realm of the Other, a trance of the hallucinatory and the ob-
scene, no less than the exalted and the edifying, he pulls together
in himself the contrarieties that are bleeding in his people and out
of them creates the resolving wholes that make those contrarie-
ties bearable. In his dark negativism, his unstanchable pessimism
regarding the race, Jeffers presents an imponderable corrective to
our ebullient optimism. But more importantly, through his own
capacity for anguish, he makes our anguish memorable. His cor-
rections are not tentative. They are, rather, efficacious because
they are realized, and as such they effect what they propose even
as they specify it.

✦

FOUR

✦

The Horseleech Hath Two Daughters

✦

The horseleech hath two daughters,
Crying, Give, give.
There are three things that are never satisfied,
Yea, four things say not, It is enough:
The grave; and the barren womb;
And the earth that is not filled with water;
And the fire that saith not, It is enough.

Proverbs 30: 15–16

✦

I. THE YEARN FOR THE ABSOLUTE

It is the paradox at the heart of the mystery of time that all du-
ration testifies chiefly to its own insufficiency. Out of all its con-
volutions, what it registers on our souls as we grow older is the
impress of timelessness. And in no other instance is this more
evident than in nature itself. "All the rivers run into the sea," saith
the Preacher, "yet the sea is not full; unto the place from whence
the rivers come, thither they return again."[1] Over the stones the
water, sucking, yearns for otherness, but that yearning is the
voice of its absolute, articulated ceaselessly as the moments fly.
Shimmering under birdflight and the drift of the leaf, the stream
scours forward over the shifting sand, funnels down the water-
course, a deeper river than water, and sifts down to a deeper ba-
sin than the sea.

It is the fluidity of nature in which this yearning is expressed
that impresses us most—it gives a haunting suavity that the me-
chanical inventions of man cannot approach. The fall of the leaf,
autumn after autumn, becomes absolutely unbearable to the soul
that has drunk deep on process. Between one's thirtieth and six-
tieth years, the years of reflection, nature makes its point and
makes it profoundly. Before that, one is mostly unconscious na-
ture itself, and after that one is something else again, either tran-
scending time or relapsing into adolescence, but in the thirty-year
span between the two, the evidence is being received, sorted, and
stored, and by the end of that period, its impress is overwhelm-
ing. The cycle of Saturn is 28 years, a cycle which defines the
larger intervals of a man's life, and by the time its course has been
twice joined, its most profound lesson has been well taught. Time
has no object that is not itself, but itself cannot answer. The purl
of the waters, the twirl of the leaf spin out the haunting litany that
each is not sufficient unto itself: the yearn for the absolute.

Perhaps the cruelest lesson of man's estrangement from nature
which city life exacts is that it deprives him of this, the deepest
teaching of nature.

The sun also ariseth
And the sun goeth down,
And hasteneth to his place where he arose.

The wind goeth toward the south
And turneth about unto the north;
It whirleth about continually,
And the wind returneth again according to his circuits.[2]

And the second lesson does not cease. No distinction can long shut it out. A man throws himself into a lofty and noble enterprise, but the rattle of hail on his shingles enforces upon his heart its witness; or a man throws himself into the arms of women, women ever younger as he ages, and yet outside his door the stream wrights in his soul the unremitting hunger—the yearn for the absolute. To live beside a river or by the sea is to be kept aware of the awesome permanence that underlies the impermanence of flux, and it is chilling.

The thing that hath been,
It is that which shall be;
And that which is done
Is that which shall be done:
And there is no new thing under the sun.[3]

Nor is the sun itself, as a symbol of permanence, any more consoling. Nothing is more annihilative than unremitting light. It falls with a consuming intensity. It burns away all but itself and even seems to devour itself when there is no check to its sources. In the lands of extreme sunlight, men and beasts creep away into any shade they can find, learn to call the absence of light blessed, and find in the beneficence of night the gratitude that Arctic wanderers confer on the sun. Wherever man turns in nature, he finds a consuming rapacity in the elements, a ravenous hunger that cannot be stanched on anything it devours. It seems to protest as it consumes that nothing is enough, that everything and anything is never enough, but must be spent in the insatiable quest for something more, something permanent.

The horseleech hath two daughters,
Crying, Give, give.
There are three things that are never satisfied,

Yea, four things say not, It is enough:
The grave; and the barren womb;
The earth that is not filled with water;
And the fire that saith not, It is enough.[4]

One retains throughout life, from instances of the greatest poignancy, this sense of the devouring transience of the experience of nature. At Stinson Beach, say, watch the wind furl the spray of the breakers and no birds in sight. Suddenly a flock of shearwaters, alternately beating their wings and gliding, veers in from over Duxbury Reef. They fly very fast, low, so low they are often hidden in the trough. Suddenly one of them dashes headlong into the water, never stopping the momentum of its flight. It is followed by another, and then another. The rest wheel, circling; and as they turn, you see the long, narrow, stiffly pointed wings, somewhat curved back, giving the unmistakable bow-and-arrow shape to the body. They are instantly joined by gulls. Cormorants arriving out of nowhere attack the fish from below, and the laboring pelicans, painfully aware of their awkwardness now as the more agile species flicker and dart, scoop up the fry from the surface. The gulls flutteringly descend on their prey, but the shearwaters plunge from full flight, surface in a moment, then momentarily stretch out their wings to get up again and be gone. Then the whole flock is suddenly out of sight.[5]

To realize how utterly attuned they are to the momentarily surfacing schools of fish leads one to wonder at their whole flight pattern, from the islands off New Zealand up the coast of Asia to the Arctic Circle, then back down the North American coast in the fall in accord with the immense pattern of the surfacing schools of fish. As the distribution of the gravel bars determines the course of the stream, so the pattern of surfacing fish might determine the life plan of the birds.

For everything hungers. What drifting plant life compels the fish to surface in their seasons, with the turning of the globe and the changing of the currents of the sea, and what mysterious pattern of fish compels the birds to make their astounding interpolar trek, some ten thousand miles in a single year? On Stinson Beach I found such a bird: the waves had caught him far from his nesting place in the south or his breeding grounds in the north. The fiercely hooked beak was still open in greed, but he hungered no more. The sea worms had taken his guts, and the shore birds his brains.

The classic meditation on time in the West was made by Saint Augustine in his *Confessions*, when for the first time the Judeo-Christian concept of God was used to establish a bearing point from which the problem could be met by recourse to a factor outside its dimension, and yet engaged through the device of introspection. In fact, Augustine's solution is that time is an activity of the mind, whereby mentality is not merely extended into the past, as memory, or into the future, as expectation, but is rather "distended," so as to hold past and future *as present.* "What then is time?" he asks in the fourteenth chapter of the eleventh book: "If no one asks me, I know; but if I want to explain it to someone who does ask me, I do not know," a remark leading his translator to exclaim that it is "one of the most effective and well known epigrams in philosophy. Augustine sums up here what Plotinus labors to express."[6] The saint continues:

Yet I state confidently that I know this: if nothing were passing away, there would be no past time, and if nothing were coming, there would be no future time, and if nothing existed, there would be no present time. How, then, can these two kinds of time, the past and the future, be, when the past no longer is, and the future as yet does not exist? But if the present were always present, and would not pass into the past, it would no longer be time, but eternity. Therefore, if the present, so as to be time, must be so constituted that it passes into the past, how can we say that it is, since the cause of its being is the fact that it will cease to be? Does it not follow that we can truly say that it is time, only because it tends toward non-being?[7]

The stream purls on its stone, the leaf whirls on its eddy of air, and the sea, revolving, works ebb tide and neap tide, and moans for what? Its own future? Its remoter past?

But how is the future, which as yet does not exist, diminished or consumed, or how does the past, which no longer exists, increase, unless there are three things in mind, which [do] all this? It looks forward [and] passes through what it considers into what it remembers. Who, then, denies that future things are not yet existent? Yet there is already in the mind an expectation of things to come. Who denies that past things no longer exist? Yet there is still in the soul the memory of past things. Who denies that present time lacks spatial extent, since it passes away in an instant? *Yet attention abides, and through it what shall be present proceeds to become something absent.* It is not, then, future time that is long, but a long future is a long expectation of the future. Nor is past time, which is not, long, but a long memory of the past.[8]

The problem is wrested from the dominance of the material or empirical dimension and interiorized in order to be posited in the true field of intellection.

Let no man tell me, then, that movements of the heavenly bodies constitute periods of time. When at the prayer of a certain man [Joshua] the sun stood still until he could achieve victory in battle, the sun indeed stood still but time went on. That battle was waged and brought to an end during its own tract of time, which was sufficient for it. Therefore, I see that time is a kind of distension. Yet do I see this, or do I only seem to my self to see it? You, O Light, will show this to me![9]

Thus the problem is not only subjectivized, where intellection can cope with it, but thrown forward upon the Absolute as well. Seen as the eternal in Greek thought, but as the personal in Hebraic and Christian thought, the recourse, if not the solution, is salvific.

But now "my years are wasted in sighs" [Psalm 30] and You, O Lord, my comfort, my Father, are eternal. But I am distracted amid times, whose order I do not know, and my thoughts, the inmost bowels of my soul, are torn asunder by tumult and change, until being purged and melted clear by the fire of your love, I may flow altogether into You.[10]

The stream purls on its stones, the leaf whirls on its unstable eddy of air, and the soul, fighting the abstraction of time like a man drowning in ether, breaks the spell of nature in a mighty yearn for the Absolute.

In his reflections on the numen, Otto speaks of the element of longing as an important aspect of the *fascinans*:

Mere love, mere trust, for all the glory and happiness they bring, do not explain to us that moment of rapture that breathes in our tenderest and most heart-felt hymns of salvation, as also in such eschatological hymns of longing as that Rhyme of St. Bernard in which the very senses seem to dance. . . . This is where the living "something more" of the *fascinans*,

the element of fascination, is to be found. It lives no less in those extol-
lings of the blessing of salvation, which recur in all religions of salvation,
and stand in such remarkable contrast to the relatively meager and fre-
quently childish import of that which is revealed in them by concept or
by image.[11]

The sense of longing that Otto considers here is omnipresent
in the work of the mature Jeffers. He aches for death with a man-
ifest and consuming hunger, though it is not felt by him, as it is
in the clear Christian hymns of expectation, uncomplicated by
pain or undistorted by dubiety. Disfigured as it is by modern
skepticism, still in Jeffers it cannot be mistaken; the longing is too
intense, too omnipresent. It breaks out in innumerable passages
in the lyrics. And it cannot remain subsumed in the implications
of the narratives, but must beat up and invest diction and rhetoric
with its urgency, as in the close of *Solstice* (which, as we saw in
Chapter 2, draws on the Medea myth), where all nature yearns
for finality, where the longing seems to swell out of the apothe-
osis of the action itself and to become a blessing.

> It snowed again and the bodies were never found. Gopher
>   and ground-squirrel
> And the rooting boar break up the sod in so many places on the high
>   hills. If the children
> Could see from where they lie hidden they'd see
> What a great surf of mountains beats from the distant ocean up to their
>   dwelling-place, wave over wave,
> Waves of live stone; and the low storm-clouds fly through the gorges
>   like hunting eagles. Or if it were summer,
> They'd see the quail and the mountain woodpecker walk above them,
>   hawks flying, and the great white clouds; they'd see
> The sea-fog drawn over the farthest ridges taut as a drum, the dry
>   white stream-beds, the strained
> Crystal of the air. It is likely the children are never able to see the wild
>   beauty of things.
> You almost think you hear them crying in the earth because the thirsty
>   roots have drunk their blue eyes.
> But no, there is not a sound.   Their mother drove east through
>   thickening phantoms
> And is thought to have died of thirst in the desert or have killed
>   herself, because she was hunted like the last wolf

And never found. Her car was found overturned in a desert gully off
    an abandoned road;
That was perhaps the place where the phantoms caught her; the
    wolf-hunt failed.
I cannot tell; I think she had too much energy to die. I think that a
    fierce unsubdued core
Lives in the high rock in the heart of the continent, affronting the
    bounties of civilization and Christ,
Troublesome, contemptuous, archaic, with thunderstorm hair and
    snowline eyes, *waiting*,
Where the tall Rockies pasture with their heads down, white-spotted
    and streaked like piebald horses, sharp withers
And thunder-scarred shoulders against the sky, standing with their
    heads down, the snow-manes blow in the wind;
But they will lift their heads and whinny when the riders come, they
    will stamp with their hooves and shake down the glaciers.[12]

Once again, I have not hesitated to instance a passage built on the
pathetic fallacy, for the longing, as Otto notes, seems to purify the
obvious sentimentality (a thing not uncommon in romantic
poetry) and thereby authenticates what rationality cannot ac-
knowledge.

Nor must it be thought that Jeffers, by restraining his longing
in such cases to the implicit, has no actual concern for anything
so specific as a doctrine of salvation. Over and over Jeffers insists,
in the most explicit way possible, that humanity can be saved. All
the great religions have spoken of the individual's need for deliv-
erance, but Jeffers, true prophet, transmutes this appeal into a
dimension that is peculiar to himself alone, characterized by his
unprecedented introduction of the perspective and vocabulary of
science to matters usually rendered from the perspective and in
the vocabulary of mysticism.

If man as a whole has become deathlike in egocentricity, for-
saking the numen for involvement with himself alone, and ne-
glecting vaster immensities, Jeffers seeks to liberate him by a rad-
ical purgation, a directing of energies not so much to what lies
above but to what lies below, a heartfelt acknowledgment of the
superiority of prime nature to the degeneracy of the human con-
dition. For Jeffers the numen is true root, and it blazes out of the
elemental. Critics like Hyatt H. Waggoner sardonically mock his
conclusions, reducing his anguished concern to mere formulae,

and making a travesty of his meaning in the process. In Waggoner's words,

> He [man] must learn, painfully and slowly to first value the hawks and the stallions above men, then to value stones above stallions and hawks. I have said above but the ladder of values leads downward, not up; the simpler the more real; the more real, the more valuable. Hawks are better than men because they are more natural; stones are more natural still. The beauty of hawks, the peace of stones, these must come to be the objects of our contemplation, but not of our desire, for to desire is to strive, and to strive is human and useless.[13]

And Kenneth Rexroth abandons his customary perspicacity to exclaim, "The constantly repeated gospel that it is better to be a rock than a man is simply an unscrupulous use of language. 'Better,' 'is,' 'man,' 'rock,' are used to promulgate an emotional falsehood, but are also used with no regard whatsoever for their actual meanings."[14]

Each, before he spoke, might well have pondered the words of Ecclesiastes, for the devaluation of value is not, of course, peculiar to Jeffers at all. Here it is canonized in Scripture:

> Wherefore I praised the dead which are already dead,
> More than the living which are yet alive.
> Yea, better is he than both they, which hath not yet been,
> Who hath not seen the evil work that is done under the sun.[15]

This Dionysiac element in the expression of devaluation is the clearest token of the presence of the numen, and it is the numen that is the key to deliverance. Seeking it, Jeffers manifests a thirst for salvation that we have to go back to the great ages of faith to match:

> Yet look: are they not pitiable? No: if they lived forever they would be
> pitiable:
> But a huge gift reserved quite overwhelms them at the end; they are
> able then to be still and not cry.
>
> And having touched a little of the beauty and seen a little of the beauty
> of things, magically grow
> Across the funeral fire or the hidden stench of burial themselves into
> the beauty they admired,
>
> Themselves into the God, themselves into the sacred steep
> unconsciousness they used to mimic

Asleep between lamp's death and dawn, while the last drunkard
    stumbled homeward down the dark street.

They are not to be pitied but very fortunate; they need no savior,
    salvation comes and takes them by force,
It gathers them into the great kingdoms of dust and stone, the blown
    storms, the stream's-end ocean.

With this advantage over their granite grave-marks, of having realized
    the petulant human consciousness
Before, and then the greatness, the peace: drunk from both pitchers:
    these to be pitied? These not fortunate?

But while he lives let each man make his health in his mind, to love the
    coast opposite humanity
And so be freed of love, laying it like bread on the waters; it is worst
    turned inward, it is best shot farthest.

Love, the mad wine of good and evil, the saint's and murderer's, the
    mote in the eye that makes its object
Shine the sun black; the trap in which it is better to catch the inhuman
    God than the hunter's own image.[16]

Perhaps we have found here as basic an explanation as we shall
ever get of the repudiation Jeffers suffered at the hands of doctri-
naire Marxists in the 1930's, or of those secularists today for
whom the new urbanization is the only solution to the problem
which confronts every generation rising upon the earth. For sal-
vation, as Otto says, is

something whose meaning is often very little apparent, is even wholly
obscure, to the "natural" man; on the contrary, so far as he understands
it, he tends to find it highly tedious and uninteresting, something down-
right distasteful and repugnant to his nature, as he would, for instance,
find the beatific vision of God in our own doctrine of salvation, or the
henosis of "God all in all" among the mystics.[17]

Be that as it may, it cannot be denied that Jeffers's inexpressible
longing for eternity invests his work with that rarest of all con-
temporary literary qualities—a profound and awe-inspiring sol-
emnity.
    For "it is not only in the religious feeling of longing," writes
Otto, "that the moment of fascination is a living factor. It is al-
ready alive and present in the moment of 'solemnity.' . . . It is
this and nothing else that in the solemn moment can fill the soul

so full and keep it so inexpressibly tranquil."[18] The note of solem-
nity is almost second nature with Jeffers, and when we focus on
him as a religious figure, we suddenly perceive that the quality
which has sometimes been put down as mere temperamental
bias, a deficiency of humor perhaps, or a disinterest in the blither
aspects of life, actually partakes of the numen. Its solemnity is
religious. Even a simple nature poem like "Evening Ebb" reveals
it:

The ocean has not been so quiet for a long while; five night-herons
Fly shorelong voiceless in the hush of the air
Over the calm of an ebb that almost mirrors their wings.
The sun has gone down, and the water has gone down
From the weed-clad rock, but the distant cloud-wall rises. The ebb
    whispers.
Great cloud-shadows float in the opal water.
Through rifts in the screen of the world pale gold gleams, and the
    evening
Star suddenly glides like a flying torch.
As if we had not been meant to see her; rehearsing behind
The screen of the world for another audience.[19]

No matter how open the vista, it is the cathedral-feeling. Every
ritual is a rehearsal behind the screen of the world for another
Audience.

In all the manifold forms in which it is aroused in us, whether in escha-
tological promise of the coming kingdom of God and the transcendent
bliss of Paradise, or in the guise of an entry into that beatific reality that
is "above the world"; whether it comes first in expectancy or pre-
intimation or in a present experience; in all these forms, outwardly di-
verse but inwardly akin, it appears as a strange and mighty propulsion
towards an ideal good known only to religion and in its nature funda-
mentally non-rational, which mind knows of in yearning and presenti-
ment, recognizing it for what it is behind the obscure and inadequate
symbols which are its only expression.[20]

    Otto goes on to show that just as the element of the mysterious
in the Wholly Other led to the supernatural and transcendent,
and that above these appeared the Beyond of mysticism through
the nonrational side of religion being raised to its highest power
and stressed to excess, so also in the case of the element of fas-
cination. At its highest point of stress, fascination becomes the

"over-abounding exuberant," a mystical moment which exactly corresponds, along this line, to the Beyond of the other line of approach. This is seen most clearly from the psychology of those great experiences—of grace, conversion, second birth—in which the religious experience appears in its pure intrinsic nature. The hard core of such experiences in their Christ-form consists of the redemption from guilt and bondage to sin. "But leaving this out of account, what we have here to point out is the unutterableness of what has been yet genuinely experienced, and how such an experience may pass into blissful excitement, rapture, and exaltation verging often on the bizarre and the abnormal."[21]

Seeking in Jeffers for an example of this "over-abounding exuberant," the higher octave of the *fascinans*, we find Orestes in the closing passages of *The Tower Beyond Tragedy* describing his conversion to Electra, who remains baffled by what she hears:

> And the gate's open, the gray boils over the
>   mountain, I have greater
> Kindred than dwell under a roof. Didn't I say this would be dark to
>   you? I have cut the meshes
> And fly like a freed falcon. To-night, lying on the hillside, sick with
>   those visions, I remembered
> The knife in the stalk of my humanity; I drew and it broke; I entered
>   the life of the brown forest
> And the great life of the ancient peaks, the patience of stone, I felt the
>   changes in the veins
> In the throat of the mountain, a grain in many centuries, we have our
>   own time, not yours; and I was the stream
> Draining the mountain wood; and I the stag drinking; and I was the
>   stars,
> Boiling with light, wandering alone, each one the lord of his own
>   summit; and I was the darkness
> Outside the stars, I included them, they were a part of me. I was
>   mankind also, a moving lichen
> On the cheek of the round stone . . . they have not made words for it,
>   to go behind things, beyond hours and ages,
> And be all things in all time, in their returns and passages, in the
>   motionless and timeless center,
> In the white of the fire[22]

Thus the yearn for the absolute becomes the vibration of the eternal, shaping the power that sustains the world. In the service of that power, Jeffers followed the numen to the end of his days, and his awe became his most pervasive intellectual attitude, not only in the writing of his books but in the guidance of his life. For his books *are* his life, and we are immeasurably the richer for that.

II. DIVINELY SUPERFLUOUS BEAUTY

Beauty is the blood of God. Like a divine emanation it infuses the substances of all animate being, as well as every inanimate thing. It is the essence of the truth that sustains the cosmos, and as such it embraces the polarities of good and evil and subsumes them into the ambiance of its total synthesis. Its essence is transformal, but it manifests itself in form.

Beauty is the blood of God in the sense that it is what the eyes behold of the life force. The great heart pumps eternally the pulsation of its infusion into contingency, the Absolute manifesting itself in powerful tidal throbs through the cosmos, interpenetrating the steeps and declivities of tangentiality, endowing every rupture and deformity with its flux of synthesis.

The blood of God both sustains and moves the cosmos. In its suffusion it fills, oceanic, the whole of reality, but riverlike it circulates and renews, highlighting in its peaked accents, shimmering across the confines and interstices of structure, sparkling and irradiating, glittering and renewing, suffusing and glowing, at once constant and changing, agitated and serene.

Beauty pulls back fragmentation from diffusion into coherence, restructures the rudimentary basis of things upon a higher principle of synthesis. The gash of violation is accommodated into the unity of its dismembered wholeness. As in birth, the rupture of forms, beauty lifts wrenched violations into totality, sinks evanescences down to subsistent concretizations, specifies in order to illuminate. A cry is heard. Out of the cry new worlds emerge, new essences proclaim their sovereignty, new hegemonies salute their destinies.

As the blood of God, beauty intoxicates as well as refreshes, maddens as well as invigorates. The excesses of God are the feminine allure of divinity, forever calling forms out of their equipoise to immolate themselves on impossible ideals that transcend their capacities, stretching the subsistent tensibility of native entities to the breaking point, eviscerating themselves upon the eventuality of a future impossible and serene. In the blood of God, beauty laughs at wounds. Out of its inexhaustible plenitude, it pumps the heartbeat of divinity. Nothing can die that is not replenishable.

"It is dislocation and detachment from the life of God that makes things ugly," wrote Emerson,[23] but in the sovereignty of beauty there is no ugliness. If beauty is in the eye of the beholder, so is ugliness, and ugliness cannot win. The eye of the beholder blinks back superficiality and distraction, focusing itself new on ever-enveloping extensions of the divine. Drawn by an unquenchable impulse, it sees through imperfection after imperfection in order to perceive the essence. All the horrors of deformation hurled by the obverse force of things cannot deflect it, nor can the superabundance of satiety fatigue it in its appetite for the ultimate. It is the unflagging demand for "More! More!" that never lets it rest. Contingency cannot contain it. It feeds on increase, and as it stanches its heart on its beatitude, it cries ever for otherness.

Boundsbreaking beauty, the blood of God, quests remorseless on its errand of reconciliation. Whatever is shattered on the flanges of opposition, of polarity, is received back upon the lave of its ministrations. Seeking out the loss of inveterate regressions, it pours into these hurts the life force of its invigoration, restoring equipoise in the vast flux of divinity. Whatever is wasted is replenished. Whatever is whole is sustained. Circling forever about the wholeness of existential reality like the Great Dragon in the cosmic life-stream, it glows and infuses its magical element.

Beauty is the blood of God, God's mother, the reason He is. All that He is and more than He is—the excesses He breathes into the manifestation of things, the divine plenitude that creates the world. In the existential instance, man's blood and God's unite to rekindle the flash, the divine spark that illuminates the darkness. But the darkness, too, is divine. In the depth of divinity shines the blood that was spent to redeem the world.

We have seen that of the divine *fascinans* both the ritualistic and the shamanistic approaches—to maintain our relation to Otto's categories—are central to the practice of Jeffers; but there is a place where both converge. Each comes together in a dimension that takes us, at last, to the very heart and center of his religious attitude, and this is the aesthetic. We have seen him identify the making of his poems as propitiary acts fulfilling the universal requirements of ritualistic religious experience, and we have seen him falter again and again before the inexpressible ecstatic moment that is the blind try for transcendence. But what the ritual is *toward*, what the *content* is of the ecstatic gasp by which he authenticates the religious experience itself, must now be established. Contained in a phrase that seems too trite to serve the tremendous implications he puts upon it, nevertheless he does not fail, from his mature conversion to the moment of his death, to affirm it: "The Beauty of God."

In the poem, "Point Pinos and Point Lobos," written in 1923, a date established by internal evidence, Jeffers formally declines the solutions of the greatest exemplars of both Western and Eastern religions—Jesus and Buddha—thereby clinching the long slow growth of his own inner awareness. He had predicted this poem in 1916, in "Ode on Human Destinies," the closing piece of *Californians*. The poem was premature, he acknowledges, written under the threat of death in World War I. Now, identifying the ultimate of things as "the beauty beyond beauty," he sees *love*, the solution of Christ, and *wisdom*, the solution of Buddha, as both missing the mark, each directed at twin aspects of contingency rather than at the Ultimate itself. He, rather, intends to pursue the thread of the beauty he sees in Nature through to the beauty that lies beyond it, an ultimacy exceeding either the love or the wisdom which, he asserts, are the most these "lords of life" can teach him:

I have spoken on sea-forelands with the lords of life, the men wisdom
     made Gods had nothing
So wise to tell me nor so sweet as the alternation of white sunlight and
     brown night,
The beautiful succession of the breeding springs, the enormous
     rhythm of the stars' deaths
And fierce renewals: O why were you rebellious, teachers of men,
     against the instinctive God,
One striving to overthrow his ordinances through love and the other
     crafty-eyed to escape them

Through patient wisdom: though you are wiser than all men you are
    foolisher than the running grass,
That fades in season and springs up in season, praising whom you
    blame.[24]

The ordinances of God, that is to say, the laws of reality, against
which he sees the two prophets as disastrously rebelling, are the
twin forces of good and evil by which God moves and sustains
and governs the universe. Perceiving that these forces are sub-
sumed in a superior principle, he concludes:

> For the essence and the end
> Of his labor is beauty, for goodness and evil are two things and still
>   variant, but the quality of life as of death and of light
> As of darkness is one, one beauty, the rhythm of that Wheel, and who
>   can behold it is happy and will praise it to the people.[25]

Earlier in the poem he had conceded that Christ knew this ab-
solute reality, the peace beyond contingency, but Jeffers declares
that Jesus forsook the Absolute to place himself in the service of
the contingent, of mankind, a lesser thing; furthermore, he re-
nounced peace for love, here defined as pity:

>   You have known this, you have
>   known peace, and forsaken
> Peace for pity, you have known the beauty beyond beauty
> And the other shore of God.[26]

Having initially envisioned the spirit of Christ as seeking
through the world always new crucifixions upon which to im-
molate itself, he predicts a time, after man has conquered inter-
planetary space ("our tributary planets tamed like the earth"),
when that spirit will make its last futile effort and will be done:

> Christ, in that moment when the hard loins of your ancient
> Love and unconquerable will crack to lift up humanity
> The last step heavenward.[27]

Then, he asks, shall God not turn and cancel out this driving am-
bition, this insane wrestling with the contingencies of good and
evil?

>   —rise and slay, and you and our children
> Suddenly stumble on peace?[28]

To describe the nature of that peace he is here seeking to pro-
claim, Jeffers turns to the traditional mystic's metaphor, the sea,
the infinity where the "chain of love" that had bound Christ to
mankind, to Contingency, falls loose:

> Ah but look seaward,
> For here where the land's charm dies love's chain falls loose, and the
>   freedom of the eyes and the fervor of the spirit
> Sea-hawks wander the huge gray water, alone in a nihilist simplicity,
>   cleaner than the primal
> Wings of the brooding of the dove on the waste of the waters
>   beginning, perplexed with creation; but ours
> Turned from creation, returned from the beauty of things to the beauty
>   of nothing, to a nihilist simplicity,
> Content with two elements, the wave and the cloud, and if one were
>   not there then the other were lovelier to turn to,
> And if neither . . .[29]

Here the poet, in the mystic's inevitable impasse with language,
can only break out in the metaphors of ecstasy in an effort to ex-
press the inexpressible:

> O shining of night, O eloquence of silence, the mother of
>   the stars, the beauty beyond beauty,
> The sea that the stars and the sea and the mountain bones of the earth
>   and men's souls are the foam on, the opening
> Of the womb of that ocean.[30]

Jeffers did not include this poem in his *Selected Poetry*, probably
for reasons of versification: it lacks the bone-cold cohesion, the
specific gravity of his best work. And indeed a certain ecstatic dif-
fuseness, typified by the long catalog of the mountains of the
world in the second part, identify it as a transitional work, falling
between his youthful and mature styles. But as a focal point in his
development, as a true crystallization point in the growth of his
consciousness, it remains crucial, perhaps the primary document
to the understanding of his religious attitude. At any rate, it is the
poem in which his intuition regarding the ultimacy of the aes-
thetic—beauty as absolute—is permanently fixed.

The importance of this recognition can hardly be overstressed.
By virtue of it, Jeffers solved the mystic's perennial impasse in re-
gard to expression. For the problem of aesthetics and mysticism
is no trifling thing, going as it does to the root of both the artistic

and the religious vocations; it has deceived many an artist and throttled many a mystic. Thus beauty has been fled from as dangerous by more than one ascetical cult. We see this explicitly in Puritanism, for instance, where beauty, as glamour, is deemed to emperil ethical values. Byzantine monasticism, moreover, is no less suspicious of it, distrusting it as allure. But for Jeffers the poet, the identification, once arrived at, meant that his contemplation and his expression were not disparate but one—simply two aspects of the same reality, the single beauty. This means that as a poet he can worship as he writes and write as he worships, and anyone who has wrestled with the problem of the religious spirit seeking expression knows that this point, once arrived at, confers tremendous deliverance, the deepest unleashing of creative powers.

Setting aside the theological problem—Jeffers's reduction of the purposes of Jesus and Buddha, which adherents of either religion would not be hard pressed to refute—the nuclear insight upon which Jeffers based his aesthetic primacy is, though more experientially than speculatively arrived at, not without philosophical support. In Scholastic philosophy, for instance, the aesthetic is predicated in man's intuition of the germ of the Absolute within the Contingent, established by virtue of the derived character of the one from the other: what we perceive as beauty is identifiable as a "participated beatitude" inherent in all contingent things by virtue of their origin in God, who keeps them in being, *sub specie aeternitatis*. The mode of this intuitive apprehension is designated as that of "connaturality," an identity of natures between subject and object, between the beholder and that which he beholds, on the basis of the universal reality which subsumes each.

Thus the tradition of Byzantine monasticism and Anglo-Saxon Puritanism, militating against beauty's allure, something dangerous and by implication evil, is derived from a practical difficulty rather than from a firm metaphysic—an error which the greater speculative resources of both the Oriental and Scholastic intellectual disciplines were able to avoid.

Ananda Coomaraswamy, in his essay "Meister Eckhart's View of Art," affirms this identity between Oriental and Occidental mysticism, insofar as the two dominant medieval traditions en-

gaged the problem of aesthetics: "The real analogy between Eck-
hart's modes of thought and those which have long been current
in India should make it easy for the Vedantist or Mahayana Bud-
dhist to understand him, which would require a much greater
effort on the part of a Protestant Christian or modern philos-
opher."[31]

Could it be that Jeffers's rejection of Christianity was actually,
for all practical purposes, seated in the anti-aesthetic, essentially
moralistic emphasis intrinsic in the Puritan spirit, of which his
natal Presbyterianism, for all its Victorian affluence, was a living
extension? If the Puritan divines who articulated the basic Prot-
estant ethic had heard what Coomaraswamy says about Eckhart's
position, they would have considered it heresy: "Art is religion,
religion, art—not related but the same."[32]

Change *art* to *beauty*, and it is Robinson Jeffers's pantheistic
credo.

So what [asks Coomaraswamy] is aesthetic experience, or, as Eckhart
calls it, recollection, contemplation, illumination (*avabhasa*), the culmi-
nating point of vision, rapture, rest? Insofar as it is accessible to a man
as rumor or foretaste, passing like a flash of lightning, it is the vision of
the world-picture as God sees it, loving all creatures alike, not as of use,
but as the image of himself in himself, each in its divine nature and in
unity, as a conscious eye situated in a mirror might see all things in all
their dimensions apart from time and space as the single object of its vi-
sion, not turning from one thing to another but seeing without light, in
a timeless image-bearing light, where "over all sensible things hangs the
motionless haze of unity." That is a seeing of things in their perfection,
ever verdant, unaged and unaging: "To have all that has being and is
lustily to be desired and brings delight; to have it all at once and whole
in the undivided soul and that in God, revealed in its perfection, in its
flower, where it first burgeons forth in the ground of its existence . . .
that is happiness," a "peculiar wonder," "neither in intellect nor will
. . . as happiness and not as intellection," not dialectically but as if one
had the knowledge and the power to gather up all time in one eternal
now, as God enjoys himself.[33]

Thus entelechy, the actualization of potentiality into the real, the
single seizure of being, true existence, God in act.

Jeffers, then, though he had to reject the Christianity he knew
to affirm it, is actually on firm metaphysical ground when, in
place of its ethical emphasis, he reasserted the primacy of the aes-

thetic. So conclusive is this certitude that it would suffice to instance the occasions, across the whole course of his creative life, by which he affirmed it. That, however, is quite unnecessary and probably, given so vast a testament, impossible. The examples available are a little less than multitudinous, for there is hardly a subject he turns his hand to but the underlying preoccupation breaks forth with passion:

> What I see is the enormous beauty of things, but what I
> attempt
> Is nothing to that. I am helpless toward that.
> It is only to form in stone the mould of some ideal humanity that
> might be worthy to *be*
> Under that lightning. Animalcules that God (if he were given to
> laughter) might omit to laugh at.
> . . .
> They are giants in agony. They have seen from my eyes
> The man-destroying beauty of the dawns over their notch yonder, and
> all the obliterating stars.
> But in their eyes they have peace. I have lived a little and I think
> Peace marrying pain alone can breed that excellence in the luckless
> race, might make it decent
> To exist at all on the star-lit stone breast.[34]

But to invoke or attest or to celebrate the beauty was, given Jeffers's basic aesthetic, plus his predilections as a poet, actually a secondary thing, though a purposive and noble one. The real core of his contemplation lay in the creative process itself, the *act* by which the beauty, the staggering and uncontainable reality of things, is registered and bodied forth. Jeffers never acknowledged this ("The poetry is in the *subject*," he insisted), but as with every great artist, his practice confirms it so that his entire body of work becomes its single and unified "instance." But what he never ceased to proclaim is the principle. Echoing Emerson's "For it is dislocation from the life of God that makes things ugly," Jeffers averred:

> Integrity is wholeness, the greatest beauty is
> Organic wholeness, the wholeness of life and things, the divine
> beauty of the universe. Love that, not man
> Apart from that, or else you will share man's pitiful confusions, or
> drown in despair when his days darken.[35]

III. THE SEX ELEMENT IN THE RELIGIOUS IDEA

The core of numinous fire investing what has been called the sex element in the religious idea inheres in the essence of procreation. The divinity raging in the sexual act is the blindness of God. Through the loins of the male and female, He creates. Blindness is the boundlessness screening the intelligence from the consequence of its need: it envelops those it engrosses in order that the frailty of reason may be overborne by the inexorable sweep of the procreative drive. Male and female fall into each other's arms, panting, embracing, mouth groping on mouth. Down below, the sexual parts rush to each other. The manflesh, erect, hungry, blazing with tensibility, plunges on target, twisting back and forth as it centers its impulse on the teleology of its need. The female response, alert, expectant, opens its orifice to catch in its rolling gyration the funneling seed. In the sexual act, men and women level themselves in order to achieve elevation. Erection topples the vertical to the horizontal in the paradox of sexuality. Instinct draws across the individual's eyes the illimitable prospect of its biological vision, a blackout. In the fall of reason the divine instance snatches its clue of immortality: "The awful daring of a moment's surrender / Which an age of prudence can never retract."[36] So God seizes his opportunities, ever watchful, gauging with ineluctable, primitive patience the moment the guard is dropped—the momentary distraction, the idle instant of unawareness, the recklessness, the risk. Through the aperture of event, the blaze of divinity breaks forth, and the seed streaks home.

The numinous core of divinity is the cry of life beyond the grave, aching for existence, the shape of the impending future clamoring to be born, beating its fists against the obdurate fact of denial. Nature screams in orgasm. The seed splurges from the seed sack of potentiality, a million spindrift offerings, each sperm streaking toward the moment of its beatitude, the syzygy of conception, engorgement in God.

At the residual base, it is simply phallus and vagina mauling each other. Drop and clutch. Suck and grab. Grunt and heave. The testes drop down to dredge up sperm and spew beatitude into the eventual. The vagina snatches marvels, sucks sperm, spume, light, fragments, splinters, makes them whole. No discrimination. Low-lunging, it grabs Godhead and ingests divinity. Semen spews. Out of the orgasm one sperm streaks and wins through. In the beatitude of the gross, Godhead shimmers. Groin to groin the sexes pummel each other; each in its own way sucks the other in.

Out of unspeakable deeps instinct struggles upward, coiling itself upon eventualities. Out of unapproachable heights, divinity drops down to engorge itself in the sentient, hungering for the grossness beyond its own definition. In the sexual act God stoops and disgorges marvels. In the cod of the male and the cleft of the female, He reconceives Himself, His feminine and masculine polarities aching into materialization, the point of consequence. Matter, flesh, is the issue between potentiality and act, between transcendence and process. Without sex, process has no recourse save repetition. It is sex that offers process divinity, enables consequence to transmute itself into recognition. For sex is the consciousness of materiality, the exclamation of self-recognition, of processive extensions.

Men and women grope through. Against a thousand resistances, a million inhibitions, against fear, prudence, awkwardness, mismatchings, flanged defections, destructive denials, they fight through. Despite themselves, despite custom, caste, organization, penitential threats, hostilities, misconceptions, they find each other. A blaze of divinity flashes between, and the instinctual impact is determined, confounding prudence.

Why does God capitalize on the excessiveness of man, maximize defection in the interest of transcendence? Why does man's intelligence cringe before the unreason of God? Why does Divinity seize its greatest opportunity in the dark convolutions of Eros? It is not that these questions have no answers. It is only that the answers leave man so little room for self-determination that he finds them unfaceable. It is at that moment of the turning of his face that the dark God pounces.

With the conclusion of the analysis of the *fascinans*, the main part of Otto's work is accomplished, and although he goes on to speak of many related things, enough has been presented, it is

hoped, to support the claim that Jeffers must be seen primarily as
a religious poet. But before leaving the subject, there is a related
aspect which Jeffers illustrates in a decisive way. It is a matter cen-
tral to the most absorbing preoccupations of our time, and its un-
derstanding will depend upon the depth with which the fore-
going considerations have been assimilated. I refer to the relation
between the erotic and the holy. Otto considers it under a sup-
plementary heading, "Analogies and Associated Feelings."

The intimate interpenetration of the non-rational with the rational ele-
ments of the religious consciousness, like the interweaving of warp and
woof in a fabric, may be elucidated by taking another familiar case, in
which a universal human feeling, that of personal affection, is similarly
interpenetrated by a likewise thoroughly non-rational and separate ele-
ment, namely, the sex instinct. It goes without saying that this latter lies
just on the opposite side of "reason" to the numinous consciousness; for,
while this is "above all reason," the sex impulse is below it, an element
in our instinctive life. "The numinous" infuses the rational from above,
"the sexual" presses up from beneath, quite wholesomely and normally
out of the nature which the human being shares with the general animal
world, into the higher realm of the specifically "humane." But though
the two things I am comparing are thus manifestly opposite extremes,
they have a closely corresponding relation to that which lies between
them, viz. the reason. For the quite special domain of the "erotic" is only
brought into existence as the reproductive instinct passes up out of the
merely instinctive life, penetrates the higher humane life of mind and
feeling, and infuses wishes, cravings, and longings in personal liking,
friendship, and love, in song and poetry and imaginative creation in gen-
eral. Whatever falls within the sphere of the erotic is therefore always a
composite product, made up of two factors: the one something that oc-
curs also in the general sphere of human behavior as such, as friendship
and liking, the feeling of companionship, the mood of poetic inspiration
or joyful exaltation, and the like; and the other an infusion of a quite spe-
cial kind, which is not to be classed with these, and of which no one can
have any inkling, let alone understand it, who have not learnt from the
actual inward experience of *eros* or love. Another point in which the
"erotic" is analogous to the "holy" is in having in the main no means of
linguistic expression but terms drawn from other fields of mental life,
which only cease to be "innocuous" (i.e., only become genuinely
"erotic" terms) when it is realized that the lover, like the orator, bard, or
singer, expresses himself not so much by the actual words he uses as by
the accent, tone, and imitative gesture which reinforce them.[37]

Otto, due perhaps to his generation, sharply distinguishes from the sexual as having a play in numinous life, which he only concedes to its composite, the erotic. But much literature since his time has opened up for us the religious dimension of sexuality itself, and in the mid-1920's, Jeffers was one of the first to accomplish this, though he has yet to be recognized for his part in it.

For in our time, when we think of the sex element in the religious idea, we think first of D. H. Lawrence, more because of his prose than his poetry. There is indeed a profound religious element in Lawrence's verse, deeply symbolic and archetypal, as seen in the poem "Snake," but for the most part his poetry is ethically oriented. Even his love poems tend to be principally concerned with the ethics of the sexual encounter between men and women. It is rare that we find in his poetry the rich evocation of the sensual flush deliberately permeated with Godhood as we are given it in "Whales Weep Not!" which will serve well enough to distinguish it from the same element when found in Jeffers:

And they rock, and they rock, through the sensual ageless ages
on the depths of the seven seas,
and through the salt they reel with drunk delight
and in the tropics tremble they with love
and roll with massive, strong desire, like gods.
Then the great bull lies up against his bride
in the blue deep of the sea,
as mountain pressing on mountain, in the zest of life:
and out of the inward roaring of the inner red ocean of whale blood
the long tip reaches strong, intense, like a maelstrom-tip, and comes to
    rest
in the clasp and the soft, wild clutch of a she-whale's fathomless body.

And over the bridge of the whale's strong phallus, linking the wonder
    of whales
the burning of archangels under the sea keep passing, back and forth,
keep passing archangels of bliss
from him to her, from her to him, great Cherubim
that wait on whales in mid-ocean, suspended in the waves of the sea
great heaven of whales in the waters, old hierarchies.
And enormous mother whales lie dreaming suckling their
    whale-tender young
and dreaming with strange whale eyes wide open in the waters of the
    beginning and the end.[38]

The correspondence here is based on the loving, tender, familial analogy to human love. For all its phallicism, it is a view of sex that is essentially maternal.

Nothing like this occurs in Jeffers. For him sex is abstract, masculine, telluric, and, especially, Uranian. In Jeffers the religious dimension is more intense. His nature is colder, and he brings the sensual permeation to bear in a much more abstract way, as a kind of metaphysical, teleological obsession. Lawrence prefers the sentient biblical flush of the *Song of Songs*, but that is something Jeffers turned from, almost deliberately, in his spiritual maturation; and once he had crossed over what must have been a distinct cleavage in his nature, a cleavage between the passionate, erotic character that can be seen in his early verse, and the cold, disdainful aloofness as it emerged in his established image, once this breakover point had occurred, one feels he took the powerful erotic element in himself and transmuted it into a distinct cosmological impress, made it function as a specific dynamic toward a transcendental and religious end. It becomes not so much the mode of the divine, as we see in traditional erotic mysticism, as an abstract element shot through the whole of reality.

It was a long time emerging in his nature, and we can see traces of the earlier, more Venusian element in the love poetry which did not get pruned from the first *Roan Stallion* volume. "Fauna" and "Mal Paso Bridge" seem terminal examples of this primary Venusian phase, but perhaps "Divinely Superfluous Beauty" is the actual breakover point, the moment at which the Venusian Eros and the more abstract Uranian aesthetic factor shortly to emerge are sustained in a kind of mutual embrace.

> The storm-dances of gulls, the barking game of seals,
> Over and under the ocean . . .
> Divinely superfluous beauty
> Rules the games, presides over destinies, makes trees grow
> And hills tower, waves fall.
> The incredible beauty of joy
> Stars with fire the joining of lips, O let our loves too
> Be joined, there is not a maiden
> Burns and thirsts for love
> More than my blood for you, by the shore of seals while the wings
> Weave like a web in the air
> Divinely superfluous beauty.[39]

The identification between sex and beauty here derives from the greater religious force that underlies both, a force to be fully developed in the narratives and meditative poems that follow.

But it is not until *Tamar* that sex as the essential revolutionary ingredient emerges to center the narrative and give the whole point its violational impact. Although sexuality permeates that entire poem, it has not yet emerged as the crucial dimension it will ultimately be. But it does partake of the divine under its negative aspects, constituting a kind of judgment on human life, breaking down human taboos and obsessions. Incest, used as the symbol of man's egocentricity, emerges as the rift upon which that self-absorption shatters. Sex is thus, as chastiser, a consuming fire, symbolic of the divine wrath.

In *The Tower Beyond Tragedy*, the incest theme was explicitly presented, perhaps because the remoteness of the Greek epoch within which the action is cast offered a more comfortable accommodation for a theme which, in a modern setting, unavoidably burns with a sensational glare. Orestes declares:

> I saw a vision of us move in the dark: all that we did or dreamed of
> Regarded each other, the man pursued the woman, the woman clung to the man, warriors and kings
> Strained at each other in the darkness, all loved or fought inward, each one of the lost people
> Sought the eyes of another that another should praise him; sought never his own but another's; the net of desire
> Had every nerve drawn to the center, so that they writhed like a full draught of fishes, all matted
> In the one mesh; when they look backward they see only a man standing at the beginning,
> Or forward, a man at the end; or if upward, men in the shining bitter sky striding and feasting,
> Whom you call Gods . . .
> It is all turned inward, all your desires incestuous, the woman the serpent, the man the rose-red cavern,
> Both human, worship forever . . .[40]

It is this perception which enables Orestes to decline the erotic, incestuous recourse which Electra offers him, the rift upon which the race is broken, accepting instead, in his famous closing peroration, a value superior to any of the attractions that obtain in humanity itself. In it Jeffers approaches, but does not yet touch, the specific ingredient of the cosmic sexual element, the element he will soon use to give his evocation of divinity a tangibility and life, a substantive factor of far greater heat than the cool purity of Orestes' vision.

For it was not until *Roan Stallion* that the archetype we are here pursuing, "the sex element in the religious idea," finds its norm in Jeffersian usage. In a single crucial passage, the relevant insight is registered, and it must be given at length, because whatever Jeffers does henceforth with sex—as primal energy, as metaphysical wrath, as analogy of divine life—in some way it always comes back to this passage. Here the cosmic sweep, the imputation of sexual energy in the delineation of abstract relationships as derived from science, is explicitly set forth. Here, one might say, was born Jeffers's Uranian view of sex, the key to his special treatment of it in the religious idea. And though other instances of analogical sexual meaning occur in his work henceforth, chiefly the telluric, nevertheless from this point on the most exalted and imaginative reach always comes back to this realization, this cosmological, essentially Uranian insight. We have instanced the same passage earlier as a paramount example of "creature-feeling," of "utter unapproachability."

It is now time to quote it in full. Situating it at the breakover point in the narrative, Jeffers takes his quarter-breed Indian woman, California, up to a mountaintop for the ritual enactment, the immolation of humanity to a power vaster than it can bear.

> Enormous films of moonlight
> Trailed down from the height. Space, anxious whiteness, vastness.
>   Distant beyond conception the shining ocean
> Lay light like a haze along the ledge and doubtful world's end. Little
>   vapors gleaming, and little
> Darknesses on the far chart underfoot symbolized wood and valley;
>   but the air was the element, the moon-
> Saturate arcs and spires of the air.
>
>   Here is solitude, here on the calvary,
>   nothing conscious
> But the possible God and the cropped grass, no witness, no eye but
>   that misformed one, the moon's past fullness.
> Two figures on the shining hill, woman and stallion, she kneeling to
>   him, brokenly adoring.

He cropping the grass, shifting his hooves, or lifting the long head to
gaze over the world,
Tranquil and powerful. She prayed aloud, "O God, I am not good
enough, O fear, O strength, I am draggled.
Johnny and other men have had me, and O clean power! Here am I,"
she said, falling before him,
And crawled to his hooves. She lay a long while, as if asleep, in reach
of the fore-hooves, weeping. He avoided
Her head and the prone body. He backed at first; but later plucked the
grass that grew by her shoulder.
The small dark head under his nostrils: a small round stone, that smelt
human, black hair growing from it:
The skull shut the light in: it was not possible for any eyes
To know what throbbed and shone under the sutures of the skull, or a
shell full of lightning
Had scared the roan strength, and he'd have broken tether, screaming,
and run for the valley.
The atom bounds-breaking,
Nucleus to sun, electrons to planets, with recognition
Not praying, self-equaling, the whole to the whole, the microcosm
Not entering nor accepting entrance, more equally, more utterly, more
incredibly conjugate
With the other extreme and greatness; passionately perceptive of
identity. . . .
The fire threw up figures
And symbols meanwhile, racial myths formed and dissolved in it, the
phantom rulers of humanity
That without being are yet more real than what they are born of, and
without shape, shape that which makes them:
The nerves and the flesh go by shadowlike, the limbs and the lives
shadowlike, these shadows remain, these shadows
To whom temples, to whom churches, to whom labors and wars,
visions and dreams are dedicate:
Out of the fire in the small round stone that black moss covered, a
crucified man writhed up in anguish;
A woman covered by a huge breast in whose mane the stars were
netted, sun and moon were his eyeballs,
Smiled under the unendurable violation, her throat swollen with the
storm and blood-flecks gleaming
On the stretched lips; a woman—no, a dark water, split by jets of
lightning, and after a season
What floated up out of the furrowed water, a boat, a fish, a
fire-globe?

It had wings, the creature,
And flew against the fountain of lightning, fell burnt out of the cloud
    back to the bottomless water . . .
Figures and symbols, castlings of the fire, played in her brain; but the
    white fire was the essence,
The burning in the small round shell of bone that black hair covered,
    that lay by the hooves on the hilltop.[41]

In introducing this example, we spoke of its primary place in
Jeffers's work, and this is true—for here the essential visionary
ingredient was first set forth, but it remains capsulated in the for-
mal narrative. It has not yet broken free to pervade the entire
work, transforming the sometimes pedestrian narrative treat-
ment we find in *Roan Stallion* into a lyric intensity. That remained
for *The Women at Point Sur*, where the total pervasion of the poetic
texture is unmistakable.

In his superb Prelude to that poem, in some ways his most
stunningly realized example of the intensity of sexual inter-
change between nature and humanity, Jeffers draws back the veil
to illuminate the psychic territory he means to explore:

In the morning
The inexhaustible clouds flying up from the south
Stream rain, the gullies of the hills grow alive, the creeks flood, the
    summer sand-bars
Burst from their mouths, from every sea-mouth wedges of yellow,
    yellow tongues. Myrtle Cartwright
Hears the steep cataracts slacken, and then thunder
Pushes the house-walls.
                    . . .
                        She opens the door on the streaming
Canyon-side, the desperate wind: the dark wet oak-leaves
All in a moment each leaf a distinct fire
Reflects the sharp flash over them: Myrtle Cartwright
Feels the sword plunge: no touch: runs tottering up hill
Through the black voice.
                    Black pool of oil hidden in the oil-tank
In Monterey felt the sword plunge: touched: the wild heat
Went mad where a little air was, metal curled back,
Fire leaped at the outlet. "Immense ages
We lay under rock, our lust hoarded,
The ache of ignorant desire, the enormous pressure,

The enormous patience, the strain, strain, the strain
Lightened we lay in a steel shell . . . what God kept for us:
Roaring marriage."
                          Myrtle Cartwright wins up hill through the
      oak-scrub
And through the rain, the wind at the summit
Knocks her breasts and her mouth, she crouches in the mud,
Feels herself four-foot like a beast and the lightning
Will come from behind and cover her, the wolf of white fire,
Force the cold flesh, cling with his forepaws. "Oh, death's
What I was after." She runs on the road northward, the wind behind
      her,
The lightnings like white doves hovering her head, harmless as
      pigeons, through great bars of black noise.
She lifts her wet arms. "Come, doves."
                               The oil-tank boils with joy in
      the north, one among ten, one tank
Burns, the nine others wait, feel warmth, dim change of patience. This
      one roars with fulfilled desire,
The ring-bound molecules splitting, the atoms dancing apart,
      marrying the air.[42]

But in the main body of *Point Sur*'s narrative, the sexual content, capitalizing upon and pursuing its *Roan Stallion* expansion to metaphysical proportions, also becomes demonic. It is constellated in the figure of a single man, the Rev. Dr. Barclay, and his psychic domination of the region is polarized in the sexual dimension. He becomes the "black Maypole," the phallic symbol around which all persons are constellated as intensely as iron filings hugging a magnet:

                Faith Heriot
Exulted and cried: "He calls the dances, he is the column,
Come up to the stone on the hill. He is what women
And drained old men want in their dreams,
What the empty bodies howl for.[43]

This motif runs through the entire last half of the poem, a demonic force that possesses everything and, like a whirlpool, draws all into its orbit.

                now the seasons turned backward
And nothing remained rational, the mad God on the hill

Possessed the region. His spirit.
                    She felt him on the stairs
In the thick dark, she felt him crowding the hallway.[44]

Its psychic polarization is explained, in a memorable aside, as the "spirit of place" possessing a man in order to find an outlet for its accumulated stress. Such possession is also seen as the crucial element in all human greatness:

He possessed all the region. His spirit.
                              It is not possible.
A man's spirit possess more than his members; but the ocean soul of
    the world
Has whirlpools in its currents, knots in the tissue, ganglia that take
Personality, make temporal souls for themselves: may parallel a man's
    before they are melted. He, fooled,
Counts his great hour, he appears to have broken his limits, imposed
    himself outward. Without subjection no Caesar,
First the subjection. Without form first no phantom. I knew that it had
    a spirit,
This coast of savage hills impendent on the ocean, insecure on the
    ocean; and few and alien
Humanity reaping it and not loving it, rape and not marriage,
Dream a bad edge on the demon. They felt it in the night
Take flesh and be man; the man imagined himself God; the people
    were fooled,
Touching reality a little, simply not geared to engage reality; the cogs
    clash and withdraw,
Some impulse was caught, the noise and the spark of the steel kissing,
    a myth and a passion.[45]

But above the regional spirit is always the vast galactic energy seeking to find a focus and an outlet:

Barclay cried on the hill, "Where does my love linger?"
A moment the mill-race of the swirling galaxy parted in his mind, he
    saw through an island of peace
That who came up to find him would go to the fires to find him, how
    could one find another on the hill,
Even God on the dark hill?[46]

Thus Barclay is always seen as the point and focus of the energy of the cosmos, parallel to the phallic lighthouse on Point Sur, which constellates the material energies of storm as he constellates the turbulence of psychic stress:

> The God in his insane mind
> Answered: "Is it nothing to you that I have given you
> The love and the power? How many times earlier in bourneless
>   eternity
> Have they not flowered; and you from the violent bath heavy with the
>   fury of the love stood evident above them,"
> He had risen and stood on the rock, "the pillar of the bride humanity's
>   desire. The explosion, the passion, repeated
> Eternally: what if they rot after, you and they shall return again. The
>   bride and the bridegroom: the unions of fire
> Like jewels on a closed necklace burn holes through extinction."[47]

The minor characters pick this obsessive religious sexuality out of the very air, echo it back in terms of their own compulsions:

> Myrtle Cartwright,
> On the dark side of the world, her face fire-brightened,
> Her eyes like red stones in the firelight: "What is the white light
> Flutters four wings in the sky, lightens from four eyes?
> The double-crested wonder, the double-throated,
> The marriage of white falcons in the height of the air,
> Here falls a feather as white as anguish.
> The daughter of man has flown from the small planet
> To be mated with God, here's a dropped flamelet.
> She is crucified in the air with kisses for nails
> Lining the palms and foot-soles, and the lance of delight,
> The dear agony of women . . ."[48]

This conceptualized analogical sexual force has always the potential for coagulation into the images of tormented carnality:

> yet passing between them
> She realized through the loathing the terrible beauty,
> The white and moulded, the hot lightnings under the cloth,
> The beastlike sucking bodies as beautiful as fire,
> The fury of archangelic passions, her eyes
> Having changed sex a moment. She whispered on the stair
> "Oh, burn, never grow old; burn, burn."[49]

All these elements are seen most deeply interwoven in the twentieth chapter where, among the women, Barclay the vision-

ary and Onorio Vasquez his prophet repolarize between them the
shifting sexual energies that saturate the universe. Barclay is
aghast that God has turned from the pure beauty of nature to love
corrupt mankind:

He has turned and left it, he has
    turned to love men,
I tell you God has gone mad, he has broken
The ring not of earth but eternity, he has broken his eternal nature: so
    a doomed man
Changes his mould of nature, a month before death, the miser scatters
    the gold counters, the coward
Eats courage somewhere. If he needed flesh
To spend that passion on . . ."
    One of the women flung herself on the rock
Under his feet, crying "Lord, I am here," and moaning anxiously. Her
    work-worn hands dug the rough stone;
Her prostrate body, ridged with the thrusting corset-bones, like a
    broken machine
Twitched out its passion.
    Barclay continued not looking downward:
    "Must he love cellular flesh, the hot quivering
Sheathed fibers, the blood in them,
And threaded lightning the nerves: had he no choice, are there not
    lions in the nights of Africa
Roar at his feet under the thunder-cloud manes? Not hawks and
    eagles, the hooked violence between
The indomitable eyes, storms of carnivorous desire drive over the huge
    blue? He has chosen insanely, he has chosen
The sly-minded, the cunning-handed, the talkative-mouthed,
The soft bodies go shelled in cloth: he has chosen to sheathe his power
    in women, sword-strike his passion
In the eyes of the sons of women. . . . I cannot tell you what madness
    covered him; he heard a girl's voice . . ." Barclay
Shook like a fire and cried out: "I am not ready to call you.
Let no one come to me, no one be moved." He stood rigid above them,
    like a man struck blind, feeling
The spheres of fire rushing through the infinite room in the bubble of
    his mind: but hearing inward his prophet
Onorio Vasquez, clamoring across the people:
"The April-eyed, the daughter," he cried in his vision,
"And the honey of God,
Walks like a maiden between the hills and high waters,

She lays her hand passing on the rock at Point Sur,
The petals of her fingers
Curve on the black rock's head, the lighthouse with lilies
Covered, the lightkeepers made drunken like bees
With her hand's fragrance . . ."
                                    Faith Heriot had come up alone,
Her laughter like a knife ran over the people, "Old Heriot
My father in the lily fragrance, the cowhide face
Drunken in the lilies." And Onorio: "I see the long thighs,
Pillars of polished lightning, the marbled flanks
That God made to desire: she is not a maiden, she is all humanity,
The breasts nippled with faces, the blue eyes
Dizzy with starlight: Oh blue wells
Of sorrow, he will brim you with rejoicing, Oh bruised lips,
The God of the stars crushed with his kiss . . ."
                                    Barclay like trumpets
Crossing a hawk's cry: "Only by force I have held off you
The meteor death plunging at the eyes that dared see and the mouth
        prophesy
What the stars cloud from. For your faith I saved you."
He said to the others: "It is true: I threw forward: He has seen.
I take youth to my age. I threw forward and struck talons in the future,
        I have spat out the mother
And left Eve in the dust of the garden. Where's Caesar, where is Jesus,
        what have I to do with dead men?
The unborn are my people and you are my people, Ah, love,
I am breeding falcons. No fear that your new lover will expiate his
        passion
On lightning-prodded Caucasus under the vultures,
On the earthquake-rocked cross. The power and the love have joined,
        the great God is the lover, he has parted the stars
Like leaves to come at love. Be silent, stand quiet, I will not have you
Move till I call." He stood rigid above them.
His arms extended and fists clenched holding them to stillness,
Holding himself; his forehead grooved with bridling
The insane starts and dispersions of his mind. Some channel
He had formed for speech: now who could remember what course
He had meant to drive the wild horses of speech?
"You straws be quiet!" There were the stars rolling enormous
Courses, the unoriented void; the explosive poison in the house
        yonder; sundown; the flurry of the nations,
But that was over: death, death? He heard Onorio moaning a vision.
        He saw Faith Heriot, white fire,

Lean into flame, he cancelled her cry with: "You here, you chosen,
Are the opening of love, you are the wedge in the block, the blast in
      the quarry, power and fire have come down to you,
This poor crack of the coast, between the ocean and the earth, on these
      bare hills. God walking in you
Goes north and gathers multitude and takes the cities to give you.
      What does he require, there is no commandment?
For love, for the broken order of the universe: nothing but acceptance.
That you *be* your desires, break custom, flame, flame,
Enter freedom."[50]

The suffusion of this underlying sexual energy to the very weft
and fabric of the narrative is unmistakable and sets *Point Sur* off
from everything that preceded it. What Jeffers discovered with
Roan Stallion is at last fully articulated, but it is not confined here.
With explosive force it casts its seminal propensity up the whole
course of his verse, to take fire in images strung almost haphaz-
ardly through the body of his narrative and lyric poems. They
burn with the greater intensity for being set against the cold dis-
dain of his established attitude.

These images are, I have suggested, both telluric and Uranian.
The telluric sexuality is seen in the earth as a reproductive being:

            There are three smoking springs in the mountain;
      here and at Big Creek and at Tassajara,
Within ten miles, besides the great guarded fountains of the south at
      Paso Robles: the earth is still young,
Hot-blooded, hot with desire, shuddering from time to time like a
      mare in heat: the mountains roar then,
There is thunder underground.[51]

Or, once again, in the analogy with the mare:

            so long an island of cloud,
Blinding white above, dark and dove-purple below, rained on a
      thousand miles of the continent's edge;
The old savage brood-mare, the earth, drank strength and forgot her
      deserts.[52]

And in a late poem where the telluric and the Uranian are
combined:

The unformed volcanic earth, a female thing,
Furiously following with the other planets

Their lord the sun: her body is molten metal pressed rigid
By its own mass; her beautiful skin, basalt and granite and the lighter
    elements,
Swam to the top. She was like a mare in her heat eyeing the stallion,
Screaming for life in the womb;
. . .
The sun heard her and stirred
Her thick air with fierce lightnings and flagellations
Of germinal power, building impossible molecules[53]

For it is chiefly the Uranian, the sky passion, articulated in beau-
tiful gouts of sexual imagery and thrown across the cosmos, that
grip his imagination. The equine figure seems to dominate both
types, but the Uranian sky-passion is nearer to the religious ele-
ment and more often gives the images of sexuality their religious
character:

and the earth, the great meteor-ball of live
    stone, flying
Through storms of sunlight as if forever, and the sun that rushes away
    we don't know where, and all
The fire-maned stars like stallions in a black pasture, each one with its
    stud of plunging
Planets for mares that he sprays with power; and universe after
    universe beyond them, all shining, all alive[54]

That from *Give Your Heart to the Hawks*. Here is another from
"Mara," where the wind as a symbol of the divine wrath finds its
sexual nexus:

Nor will he feel the wind,
Nor taste the rain, nor see again the great crowning beauty of the year,
    that southeast storm
In the week of Christmas or New Year's, when the wind tugs the roof
    like a righteous man
Lifting his unfaithful wife by the hair
From the bed to the door, and under a roaring blue-black sky the black
Ocean flames all over with flying white foam,
And no bird flies.[55]

Less powerful but still indicative is this passage from a poem
whose title, "Resurrection," shows the author's real preoccupa-
tion in its unfolding:

They went out together,
And down the gross darkness of the night mountain. They were rather
    like one star than two people, for that night at least,
So love had joined them to burn a moment for each other, no other star
    was needed in all the black world.[56]

Sometimes it takes on a more mythical dimension, in keeping
with a change of situation and theme, but it is there nevertheless.
This from "At the Fall of an Age":

Roar in the night, storm, like a lion, spare not the stars.
They have planted wild seed in the air who lifted God's
Daughter on high, wavering aloft, blessing the new
Age at birth with the beauty of her body . . .[57]

But then it bursts out again in the original Uranian vision:

Then, yellow dawn
Colors the south, I think about the rapid and furious lives in the sun:
They have little to do with ours; they have nothing to do with oxygen
    and salted water; they would look monstrous
If we could see them: the beautiful passionate bodies of living flame,
    batlike flapping and screaming,
Tortured with burning lust and acute awareness, that ride the storm-
    tides
Of the great fire-globe.[58]

And again:

There is another nature of fire; not the same fire,
But fire's father: "Holy, holy, holy,"
Sing the angels of the sun, pouring out power
On the lands and the planets; but it's no holier
Than a fire in a hut, it is another chemistry,
More primitive, more powerful, more universal, power's peak,
The fire of the sun and stars and the pale sheet-fire
Of a far-off nebula, a mist-fleck at midnight
In the infinite sky; a sworl of a million million suns, dragging their
    satellites
Like dark women by the hair
Through the wild acre.[59]

This rich vein of Uranian sexuality in the writings of Jeffers sets
his poetry apart from all contemporary verse and, by elevating
that tremendous source of energy to the transcendent, strength-

ens his great claim to religious consideration. Nor does its use in this regard stop there; its resonance extends back from the very root of our obsession, of which it is actually the higher octave: the problem of violence. Groping into that mystery, we may yet discover (in his confrontation of it) not indeed its solution, which can only be found on the Cross, but certainly its substance, its contours, and its divine vibration.

> The pure air trembles, O pitiless God,
> The air aches with flame on these gaunt rocks
> Over the flat sea's face, the forest
> Shakes in gales of piercing light.
>
> But the altars are behind and higher
> Where the great hills raise naked heads,
> Pale agonists in the reverberance
> Of the pure air and the pitiless God.
>
> On the domed skull of every hill
> Who stand blazing with spread vans,
> The arms uplifted, the eyes in ecstasy?
>
> What wine has the God drunk, to sing
> Violently in heaven, what wine his worshippers
> Whose silence blazes? The light that is over
> Light, the terror of noon, the eyes
> That the eagles die at, have thrown down
> Me and my pride, here I lie naked
> In a hollow of the shadowless rocks,
> Full of the God, having drunk fire.[60]

✦

Conclusion

This essay was begun as a venture in classification: an attempt to determine the character of a writer who, though indubitably of the genus *poetas*, has never been satisfactorily defined as to species. None of the categories proposed have seemed adequate; *poetas philosophicus*, heretofore the most generally employed, lacks conviction by virtue of a terminal deficiency in the special function of the activity proposed. We, therefore, in its place proposed the category *religiosus* as constituting the more satisfactory, and hence the truer, definition—and urge its recognition. The factors preventing this identification earlier may be attributed to the contemporary spiritual crisis obtaining at the moment of the author's emergence, obscured by his hostility to institutional religions *per se*, to his violation of conventional religious attitudes, to his attacks upon the moral and ethical foundations of the prevalent religious sentiment of his time, to his inflammatory preoccupation with violence, cruelty, and the disruptive power of sex, and to his reductive metaphysical annulment of all things to a "nihilistic simplicity."

In order to substantiate the category, we have had recourse to one of the basic texts of the twentieth-century religious revision, Rudolf Otto's *The Idea of the Holy*, and by equating examples from the poet's work with the various aspects of the holy as that author analyzes them, we have shown that far from being antireligious, as originally charged, this poet is rather a radical example of the breed—radical in the etymological sense of a return to the roots. This poet, it would seem, is not less but more intensely religious than his contemporaries, and he is so precisely by reason of his passion to resecure for humanity that root, that underlying nerve, of primordial religious response.

But in attempting to solve the problem of mere classification, we hope that something more has been realized. We hope that by striking to the central core of his motivation, we have released a

comprehensible light that will flow upward and outward and il-
lumine the structure of the total achievement, so that the man will
emerge in a more positive, a more powerful light, and both poetry
and religion will be seen to fuse in that dimension wherein each
has always found its maximum point focus: prophecy.

As prophet, the religious poet transcends his category—a fac-
tor which we are now able to acknowledge in the case of Blake,
though his own time denied it. Blake's defects as a poet are more
and more felt to be subsumed in the overmastering force of his
prophetic vision. We are beginning to see the same acknowledg-
ment in the case of Whitman, whose limitations, so recently the
object of denigration, are more and more acknowledged to be in-
gredients in essential poetic function—they are becoming "al-
lowed" by virtue of the revelatory insights his once outrageous
freedom of expression seemed to deny him.

As prophet, Jeffers has set his face stonelike against the same
future that Whitman, likewise as prophet, hailed. Only the future
will decide between them, will determine which was right, which
wrong. But as to the religious dimension, there can be no doubt
that Jeffers, considered in the light of the essential archetype as
Rudolf Otto analyzed it, is by far the more concentrated specimen
of the species, the more *pure* example of *poetas religiosus*. What he
lacks in devotional decorum he makes up for in the astonishing
intensity of this primitivistic force, his grasp of the power, the
wonder, the awe of a God palpably immediate yet unalterably be-
yond science's continuing probe of the cosmos. In this he fulfills
the words of a contemporary anthologist, R. S. Thomas, who in
his introduction to the *Penguin Book of Religious Verse* writes:

What is the common ground between religion and poetry? Is there such?
Do definitions help? If I say that religion is the total response of the whole
person to reality, but poetry the response of a certain kind of person, I
appear to be doing so at the expense of poetry. Perhaps Coleridge can
help here. The nearest we approach to God, he appears to say, is as cre-
ative beings. The poet, by echoing the primary imagination, recreates.
Through his work he forces those who read him to do the same, thus
bringing them nearer to the primary imagination themselves, and so, in
a way, nearer to the actual being of God as displayed in action. So Cole-
ridge in the thirteenth chapter of his *Biographia Literaria*. Now the power
of the imagination is a unifying power, hence the force of metaphor; and

the poet is the supreme manipulator of metaphor. This would dispense of him as a minor craftsman among many. The world needs the unifying power of the imagination. The two things which give it best are poetry and religion. Science destroys as it gives.[1]

If it does, it finds its gifts restored again in the poetry of Jeffers, no enemy of science, who reconstitutes, in the unifying symbols of his metaphors, the vast context of the cosmos that science has opened to the eyes of man. Loving it, he unifies it; fearing it, he reveals its wrath and its awe; worshipping it, he establishes it as the very throne of that unspeakable God who transcends it in excess even as He sustains it in being. It is in the celebration of the divine excess that Jeffers tacitly acknowledges the limitation of his avowed pantheism and places himself among the vast company of mystics and prophets and poets of all ages and all faiths— those who have seen to the plenitude beyond the registration of power, the vast and abstract reality that lies beyond nature, to the verifiable face of HIM WHO IS.

✦

The Poet Is Dead

✦

A MEMORIAL FOR
ROBINSON JEFFERS
1887–1962

✦

To be read with a full stop between the strophes,
as in a dirge.

In the evening the dusk
Stipples with lights. The long shore
Gathers darkness in on itself
And goes cold. From the lap of silence
All the tide-crest's pivotal immensity
Lifts into the land.

*

Snow on the headland,
Rare on the coast of California.
Snow on Point Lobos,
Falling all night,
Filling the creeks and the back country,
The strangely beautiful
Setting of death.

*

For the poet is dead.
The pen, splintered on the sheer
Excesses of vision, unfingered, falls.
The heart-crookt hand, cold as a stone,
Lets it go down.

*

The great tongue is dried.
The teeth that bit to the bitterness
Are sheathed in truth.

*

If you listen
You can hear the field mice
Kick little rifts in the snow-swirls.
You can hear
Time take back its own.

*

For the poet is dead.
On the bed by the window,
Where dislike and desire
Killed each other in the crystalline interest,
What remains alone lets go of its light. It has found
Finalness. It has touched what it craved: the passionate
Darks of deliverance.

*

At sundown the sea wind,
Burgeoning,
Bled the west empty.

*

Now the opulent
Treacherous woman called Life
Forsakes her claim. Blond and a harlot
She once drank joy from his narrow loins.
She broke his virtue in her knees.

*

In the water-gnawn coves of Point Lobos
The white-faced sea otters
Fold their paws on their velvet breasts
And list waveward.

*

But he healed his pain on the wisdom of stone.
He touched roots for his peace.

*

The old ocean boils its wrack,
It steeps its lees.

*

For the poet is dead. The gaunt wolf
Crawled out to the edge and died snapping.
He said he would. The wolf
Who lost his mate. He said he would carry the wound,
The blood-wound of life, to the broken edge
And die grinning.

*

Over the salt marsh the killdeer,
Unrestrainable,
Cry fear against moonset.

*

And all the hardly suspected
Latencies of distintegration
Inch forward. The skin
Flakes loss. On the death-gripped feet
The toenails glint like eyeteeth
From the pinched flesh.
The caged ribs and the bladed shoulders,
Ancient slopes of containment,
Imperceptibly define the shelves of structure,
Faced like rock ridges

Boned out of mountains, absently revealed
With the going of the snow.

*

In the sleeve of darkness the gopher
Tunnels the sod for short grass
And pockets his fill.

*

And the great phallus shrinks in the groin,
The seed in the scrotum
Chills.

*

When the dawn comes in again,
Thoughtlessly,
The sea birds will mew by the window.

*

For the poet is dead. Beyond the courtyard
The ocean at full tide hunches its bulk.
Groping among the out-thrusts of granite
It moans and whimpers. In the phosphorescent
Restlessness it chunks deceptively,
Wagging its torn appendages, dipping and rinsing
Its ripped sea rags, its strip-weeded kelp.
The old mother grieves her deathling.
She trundles the dark for her lost child.
She hunts her son.

*

On the top of the tower
The hawk will not perch tomorrow.

*

And on surf-swept Point Lobos the cypresses
Stagger in the wind, incestuous
Siblings of the drift. Flexed in transgression
The clenched limbs of lovers press vein to vein,
The seethe of their passion
Scrawling a stark calligraphy on the palimpsest of night,
Etched with the swan skein and the leaf,
Impalpably mutable, the gnomic
Marginalia of death.

*

But in the gorged rivermouth
Already the steelhead fight for entry.
They feel fresh water

Sting through the sieves of their salt-coarsened gills.
They shudder and thrust.

      *

So the sea broods. And the aged gull,
Asleep on the water, too stiff to feed,
Spins in a side-rip crossing the surf
And drags down.

      *

This mouth is shut. I say
The mouth is clamped cold.
I tell you this tongue is dried.

      *

But the skull, the skull,
The perfect sculpture of bone!—
Around the forehead the fine hair,
Composed to the severest
Lineaments of thought,
Is moulded on peace.

      *

And the strongly-wrought features,
That keep in the soul's serenest achievement
The spirit's virtue,
Set the death mask of all mortality,
The impress of that grace.

      *

In the shoal-champed breakers
One wing of the gull
Tilts like a fin through the ribbon of spume
And knifes under.

      *

And all about there the vastness of night
Affirms its sovereignty. There's not a cliff
Of the coastline, not a reef
Of the waterways, from the sword-thrust Aleutians
To the scorpion-tailed stinger Cape Horn—
All that staggering declivity
Grasped in the visionary mind and established—
But is sunken under the dark ordainment,
Like a sleeper possessed, like a man
Gone under, like a powerful swimmer
Plunged in a womb-death washed out to sea
And worked back ashore.

      *

The gull's eye
Skinned to the wave, retains the ocean's
Imponderable compression,
And burns yellow.

*

The poet is dead. I tell you
The nostrils are narrowed. I say again and again
The strong tongue is broken.

*

But the owl
Quirks in the cypresses, and you hear
What he says. He is calling for something.
He tucks his head for his mate's
Immemorial whisper. In her answering voice
He tastes the grace-note of his reprieve.

*

When fog comes again to the canyons
The redwoods will know what it means.
The giant sisters
Gather it into their merciful arms
And stroke silence.

*

You smell pine resin laced in the salt
And know the dawn wind has veered.

*

And on the shelf in the gloom,
Blended together, the tall books emerge,
All of a piece. Transparent as membranes
The thin leaves of paper hug their dark thoughts.
They know what he said.

*

The sea, reaching for life,
Spits up the gull. He falls spread-eagled,
The streaked wings swept on the sand.
Vague fingers of snow, aimlessly deft, grope for his eyes.
When the blind head snaps
The beak krakes at the sky.

*

Now the night closes.
All the dark's negatory
Decentralization
Quivers toward dawn.

*

He has gone into death like a stone thrown in the sea.
                    *

And in far places the morning
Shrills its episodes of triviality and vice
And one man's passing. Could the ears
That hardly listened in life
Care much less now?
                    *

Snow on the headland,
The strangely beautiful
Oblique concurrence,
The strangely reticent
Setting of death.
                    *

The great tongue
Dries in the mouth. I told you.
The voiceless throat
Cools silence. And the sea-granite eyes.
Washed in the sibilant waters
The stretched lips kiss peace.
                    *

The poet is dead.
                    *

Nor will ever again hear the sea lions
Grunt in the kelp at Point Lobos.
Nor look to the south when the grunion
Run the Pacific, and the plunging
Shearwaters, insatiable,
Stun themselves in the sea.

Notes

✦

Notes

INTRODUCTION

1. Quoted in S. S. Alberts, *A Bibliography of the Works of Robinson Jeffers* (New York, 1933), p. 231.
2. Ibid.
3. "Symbolic Themes" published as Robert J. Brophy, *Robinson Jeffers: Myth, Ritual, and Symbol in his Narrative Poems* (Cleveland, Ohio, 1973); Ann N. Ridgeway, *The Selected Letters of Robinson Jeffers, 1897–1962* (Baltimore, Md., 1968); Brother Antoninus, *Robinson Jeffers: Fragments of an Older Fury* (Berkeley, Calif., 1968).
4. Mercedes Monjian, *Robinson Jeffers: A Study in Inhumanism* (Pittsburgh, Penn., 1958).
5. Radcliffe Squires, *The Loyalties of Robinson Jeffers* (Ann Arbor, Mich., 1956).
6. Frederic Carpenter, *Robinson Jeffers* (New York, 1962), p. 109.
7. Brophy, *Robinson Jeffers*; Bill Hotchkiss, *Jeffers: The Sivastic Vision* (Newcastle, Calif., 1975). Since this chapter was written, a full-scale study of the poet's religious thought has appeared: Marlan Beilke, *Shining Clarity: God and Man in the Works of Robinson Jeffers* (Amador City, Calif., 1977).
8. Hyatt Howe Waggoner, *The Heel of Elohim* (Norman, Okla., 1950), pp. 131–32.
9. Carpenter, *Jeffers*, p. 116.
10. Monjian, *Jeffers: A Study*, p. 89.
11. Rudolf Otto, *The Idea of the Holy* (London, 1923), p. 5.
12. Ibid.
13. Ibid., p. 6.
14. Ibid., p. 12.
15. Mircea Eliade, *Myths, Dreams, and Mysteries* (New York, 1957), p. 124.
16. Ibid.
17. Ibid., p. 125.

ONE

1. Amos Wilder, *The Spiritual Aspects of the New Poetry* (New York, 1940), p. 141.
2. Ibid.
3. *Encyclopedia Americana* (New York, 1963), vol. 21, p. 249.

4. Mircea Eliade, *Myths, Dreams, and Mysteries* (New York, 1957), p. 124.

5. *Catholic Encyclopedia* (New York, 1967), vol. 10, s.v. "Pantheism" (pp. 947–50).

6. Robinson Jeffers, "The Poet in Democracy," published as *Themes in My Poems* (The Book Club of California, 1956), but cited here from Melba Berry Bennett, *The Stone Mason of Tor House* (Los Angeles, 1966), p. 182; Bennett works from Jeffers's original manuscript rather than from the revised published version.

7. *Catholic Encyclopedia*, s.v. "Pantheism."

8. *Encyclopedia Americana*, vol. 21, p. 249.

9. Rudolf Otto, *The Idea of the Holy* (London, 1923), p. 10.

10. Ibid., p. 9.

11. Job 40:4

12. Robinson Jeffers, *The Selected Poetry of Robinson Jeffers* (New York, 1933), p. 174; hereafter cited as *SP*.

13. Robinson Jeffers, *Be Angry at the Sun* (New York, 1941), p. 29.

14. *SP*, pp. 185–86.   15. *SP*, p. 186.

16. *SP*, pp. 186–87.   17. *SP*, pp. 260–61.

18. *SP*, p. 167.   19. Otto, *Idea*, p. 12.

20. Ibid.   21. Ibid.

22. Ibid., p. 13.   23. Ibid.

24. Unfortunately, I have been unable to locate my source for this quotation.

25. *SP*, pp. 423–24.

26. Robinson Jeffers, *Dear Judas and Other Poems* (New York, 1929), p. 32.

27. Ibid., pp. 32–33.   28. *SP*, pp. 145–46.

29. *SP*, pp. 189–91.   30. *SP*, pp. 203–4.

31. *SP*, p. 204.   32. *SP*, p. 204.

33. Otto, *Idea*, p. 19.   34. Ibid., p. 15.

35. Ibid., p. 16.   36. Ibid.

37. Ibid.

38. Frederic Carpenter, *Robinson Jeffers* (New York, 1962), p. 112.

39. Robinson Jeffers, *Hungerfield and Other Poems* (New York, 1954), p. 96.

40. Ibid., pp. 9–10.

41. Ibid., pp. 10–12.

42. Robinson Jeffers, *Roan Stallion, Tamar and Other Poems* (New York, 1925), p. 93.

43. Otto, *Idea*, p. 17.   44. *SP*, p. 159.

45. *SP*, p. 159.   46. "Hellenistics," in *SP*, p. 602.

47. *SP*, pp. 152–53.

TWO

1. Radcliffe Squires, *The Loyalties of Robinson Jeffers* (Ann Arbor, Mich., 1956), pp. 1–2.

2. Frederick Lewis Allen, *Only Yesterday* (New York, 1964), pp. 233–34.

3. Squires, *Loyalties*, p. 4.

4. David Littlejohn, "Cassandra Grown Tired," *Commonweal*, Dec. 7, 1962, p. 276.

5. Ibid., pp. 277–78.

6. Robinson Jeffers, "To the Stone-Cutters," in *The Selected Poetry of Robinson Jeffers* (New York, 1933), p. 84; *Selected Poetry* hereafter cited as *SP*.

7. *SP*, pp. 114–15.

8. Robinson Jeffers, "Cassandra," in *The Double Axe* (New York, 1948), p. 117.

9. Robinson Jeffers, *Solstice and Other Poems* (New York, 1935), p. 94.

10. Robinson Jeffers, *The Women at Point Sur* (New York, 1927), pp. 36–37.

11. Ibid., p. 118.

12. Ibid., p. 119.

13. Rudolf Otto, *The Idea of the Holy* (London, 1923), p. 18.

14. Robinson Jeffers, "The Humanist's Tragedy," in *Dear Judas and Other Poems* (New York, 1929).

15. Mircea Eliade, *The Sacred and the Profane* (New York, 1959), pp. 11–12.

16. Robinson Jeffers, *Medea* (New York, 1946), pp. 90–91.

17. Jeffers, *Solstice*, p. 106.   18. Ibid., p. 112.

19. Ibid., p. 130.   20. Ibid., pp. 131–32.

21. *SP*, p. 360.   22. Jeffers, *Point Sur*, pp. 97–98.

23. Ibid., pp. 98–99.   24. *Tamar, SP*, pp. 28–29.

25. Jeffers, *Point Sur*, pp. 114–15.   26. Ibid., p. 165.

27. Robinson Jeffers, *Cawdor and Other Poems* (New York, 1928), p. 109.

28. Robinson Jeffers, *Hungerfield and Other Poems* (New York, 1954), p. 84.

29. Otto, *Idea*, p. 19.

30. *SP*, p. 473.

31. Yvor Winters, *In Defense of Reason*, 3d ed. (Denver, 1947), p. 33.

32. Jeffers, *Hungerfield*, p. 23.

33. *SP*, p. 357.

34. George Lamb, "Love and Violence in the Apocalypse," in *Love and Violence*, ed. P. Bruno de Jesus-Marie, O.D.C. (New York, 1954), p. 250.

35. Ibid., p. 259.   36. Ibid.

37. Otto, *Idea*, p. 19.   38. Ibid., p. 20.

39. Ibid., p. 21.

40. Frederic Carpenter, *Robinson Jeffers* (New York, 1962), p. 133.

41. *SP*, pp. 365–66, 370–71.   42. *SP*, p. 371.

43. *SP*, p. 593.   44. Otto, *Idea*, p. 21.

45. Jeffers, *Point Sur*, p. 103.   46. *SP*, pp. 558–59.

47. Robert Martin Adams, *Nil* (New York, 1966), p. 3.

48. Ibid.   49. Ibid., p. 6.

50. Eliade, *Sacred*, p. 202.   51. Ibid.

52. Otto, *Idea*, pp. 26, 28.
53. Ibid., p. 29.
54. Ibid., p. 30.
55. Ibid.
56. *SP*, p. 40.
57. *SP*, pp. 138–39.
58. Jeffers, *Point Sur*, p. 30.
59. Ibid.
60. Ibid., p. 170.
61. Jeffers, *Double Axe*, p. 92.
62. Ibid., pp. 92–93.
63. Ibid., p. 93.
64. Ibid., pp. 93–94.
65. Ibid., p. 94.

THREE

1. Song of Solomon 8: 2–3.
2. Louis Lavelle, *The Meaning of Holiness* (New York, 1954), p. 3.
3. Rudolf Otto, *The Idea of the Holy* (London, 1923), p. 31.
4. Ibid.
5. Robinson Jeffers, *The Selected Poetry of Robinson Jeffers* (New York, 1933), p. 153; hereafter cited as *SP*.
6. *SP*, pp. 152–53.
7. Otto, *Idea*, p. 31.
8. *SP*, pp. 158–60.
9. *SP*, pp. 502–3.
10. *SP*, pp. 605–6.
11. "At the Birth of an Age," in *SP*, p. 551.
12. "Self-Criticism in February," in *SP*, p. 601.
13. Mircea Eliade, *Cosmos and History* (New York, 1954), p. 5.
14. Otto, *Idea*, p. 33.
15. Robinson Jeffers, *Be Angry at the Sun* (New York, 1941), pp. 111–13.
16. *SP*, p. 175.
17. *SP*, p. 83.
18. *SP*, p. 15.
19. Robinson Jeffers, *The Women at Point Sur* (New York, 1927), pp. 72–73.
20. Andreas Lommel, *Shamanism: The Beginning of Art* (New York, 1967), pp. 29, 151.
21. James Joyce, *Portrait of the Artist as a Young Man*, Modern Library ed. (New York, 1928), p. 299.
22. Lommel, *Shamanism*, p. 10.
23. Ibid.
24. Unfortunately, I am unable to identify the source of this song.
25. Lommel, *Shamanism*, p. 75.
26. Ibid., p. 49.
27. Robinson Jeffers, *The Beginning and the End* (New York, 1963), p. 62.
28. Quoted in *The Exacting Ear*, ed. Eleanor McKinney (New York, 1966), p. 96.
29. Otto, *Idea*, p. 33.
30. *SP*, p. 34.
31. John G. Neihardt, *Black Elk Speaks* (Lincoln, Neb., 1961), p. 18.
32. *SP*, pp. 221–22.

33. *SP*, pp. 248–49. 34. *SP*, pp. 249–50.
35. *SP*, p. 250. 36. *SP*, pp. 113–14.
37. Jeffers, *Point Sur*, pp. 101–2. 38. *SP*, pp. 229–30.
39. Robinson Jeffers, *Such Counsels You Gave to Me* (New York, 1937), pp. 60–61.
40. Otto, *Idea*, p. 33.
41. Ibid., p. 34.
42. Robinson Jeffers, *Roan Stallion, Tamar and Other Poems* (New York, 1925), pp. 242–43.
43. *SP*, p. 160. 44. *SP*, p. 139.
45. *SP*, p. 153. 46. *SP*, pp. 249–50.

FOUR

1. Ecclesiastes 1:7. 2. Ecclesiastes 1:5–6.
3. Ecclesiastes 1:9. 4. Proverbs 30:15–16.
5. Adapted from "Birds of the Jeffers Country," by Laidlaw Williams, *Carmelite*, Dec. 12, 1928, p. 10.
6. *The Confessions of Saint Augustine*, trans. John K. Ryan (New York, 1960), pp. 287, 410n.
7. Ibid., p. 287. 8. Ibid., p. 301.
9. Ibid., p. 296. 10. Ibid., p. 302.
11. Rudolf Otto, *The Idea of the Holy* (London, 1923), p. 34.
12. Robinson Jeffers, *Solstice & Other Poems* (New York, 1935), pp. 130–32.
13. Hyatt H. Waggoner, *The Heel of Elohim* (Norman, Okla., 1950), p. 111.
14. Kenneth Rexroth, *Assays* (New York, 1961), p. 214.
15. Ecclesiastes 4:2–3.
16. Robinson Jeffers, "Meditation on Saviors," in *The Selected Poetry of Robinson Jeffers* (New York, 1933), pp. 203–4; *Selected Poetry* hereafter cited as *SP*.
17. Otto, *Idea*, p. 35. 18. Ibid.
19. *SP*, p. 263. 20. Otto, *Idea*, p. 36.
21. Ibid., p. 37. 22. *SP*, pp. 138–39.
23. Ralph Waldo Emerson, *The Selected Writings* (New York, 1940), p. 328.
24. Robinson Jeffers, *Roan Stallion, Tamar and Other Poems* (New York, 1925), p. 241.
25. Ibid. 26. Ibid., p. 236.
27. Ibid., p. 237. 28. Ibid.
29. Ibid., p. 236. 30. Ibid.
31. Ananda K. Coomaraswamy, *The Transformation of Nature in Art* (Cambridge, Mass., 1934), p. 61.
32. Ibid., p. 62.
33. Ibid., p. 93.
34. "An Artist," in *SP*, pp. 193–94.

35. "The Answer," in *SP*, p. 594.
36. T. S. Eliot, *The Waste Land and Other Poems* (New York, 1930), p. 45.
37. Otto, *Idea*, p. 46.
38. D. H. Lawrence, *The Complete Poems of D. H. Lawrence*, 2 vols., Vivian DeSola Pinto and F. Warren Roberts, eds. (New York, 1964), p. 694. © 1964, 1971 by Angelo Ravagli and C. M. Weekley, executors of the estate of Frieda Lawrence Ravagli. All rights reserved. Reprinted by permission of Viking-Penguin, Inc., and Laurence Pollinger Ltd.
39. *SP*, p. 65.
40. *SP*, p. 138.
41. *SP*, pp. 152–54.
42. Robinson Jeffers, *The Women at Point Sur* (New York, 1927), pp. 15–17.

43. Ibid., p. 164.
44. Ibid., p. 137.
45. Ibid., pp. 133–34.
46. Ibid., p. 154.
47. Ibid., pp. 102–3.
48. Ibid., p. 169.
49. Ibid., p. 97.
50. Ibid., pp. 117–21.

51. Jeffers, *Solstice*, pp. 99–100.
52. *Thurso's Landing*, in *SP*, p. 338.
53. Robinson Jeffers, "The Beginning and the End," in *The Beginning and the End* (New York, 1963), p. 5.
54. *SP*, p. 429.
55. Robinson Jeffers, *Be Angry at the Sun* (New York, 1941), pp. 64–65.
56. Robinson Jeffers, *Give Your Heart to the Hawks* (New York, 1933), p. 175.
57. *SP*, p. 504.
58. Robinson Jeffers, "Animals," in *Hungerfield and Other Poems* (New York, 1954), p. 106.
59. "Fire," in *Hungerfield*, p. 103.
60. Robinson Jeffers, "Noon," in *Roan Stallion, Tamar & Other Poems*, Modern Library ed. (New York, 1935), p. 291.

CONCLUSION

1. R. S. Thomas, *The Penguin Book of Religious Verse* (Baltimore, Md., 1963), p. 8.

Index

Absolute (the): overpoweringness of, 74–75; the yearn for, 129–40; Christ and (Jeffers on), 143–45. *See also* Awe; God; Wrath
Adams, Robert Martin, 80–81
Aesthetics, mysticism and, 144–47, 152
Alberts, S. S., 1
Allen, Frederick Lewis, 49–50
"Animals," 164
"Answer, The," 147
"Antrim," 69–70
"Apology for Bad Dreams," 19, 108–9
Archetypes, 25, 59–60, 62, 99, 104, 106, 109, 113, 154, 168
Ark of the Covenant, 57–58
"Artist, An," 116, 147
Astronomy, 3, 14, 76, 120–21
Atheists, 36–37
"At the Birth of an Age," 79, 103, 123
"At the Fall of an Age," 101–2, 164
Augustine, Saint, 132–33
"Autumn Evening," 22–23
Awe, religious, 11, 14–15, 17, 23, 36–39, 44–45, 103, 140, 168f. *See also* Dread; *Mysterium tremendum*; Wrath

Beauty, divine, 140–48
"Beginning and the End, The," 162–63
Black Elk, 117
Blake, William, 168
"Bowl of Blood, The," 108, 123

"Broken Balance, The," 21
Brophy, Robert J., 3
Buddhism, 68, 81, 142, 145f
Burke, Kenneth, 80
Byzantine monasticism, 145

Californians, 142
Carpenter, Frederic, 3f, 39, 75
"Cassandra," 53
Cawdor, 20–21, 66–67, 115
Christ, Jesus: Jeffers and, 6, 29–31, 32, 142–47; God in, 8, 14f, 74. *See also* God
Coleridge, S. T., 168
"Come, Little Birds," 40, 107–8
Confessions (Augustine), 132
Consciousness: movements exploring, 5–6; beginning of, 57; radical, 74, 167. *See also* Creature-consciousness; Numinous states
"Continent's End," 101
Coomaraswamy, Ananda, 145–46
Copernicus, 14
Creature-consciousness, 11–23, 24, 45, 76
Cretan Woman, The, 58, 67

Dear Judas, 29–31, 32
Death: in *Hungerfield*, 40–43; Medea's, 60–62; lives worse than, 61; Jeffers's longing for, 134–40, 142
Deliverance, *see* Salvation
Demonic dread, *see* Dread
Dionysus, 58, 99, 102, 136

Divine (the), *see Fascinans*; God
"Divinely Superfluous Beauty,"
  152–53
Dread, demonic, 36–46, 98
"Drunken Charlie," 123

Ecclesiastes, 130, 136
Einstein, Albert, 14
Eliade, Mircea, 7–8, 14, 58f, 81ff,
  106
Emerson, Ralph Waldo, 12–13,
  141, 147
Erotic (the), *see* Sex
"Evening Ebb," 138
Excessiveness, in Jeffers's work,
  43–44, 70–71, 95, 108

Fascinans, the divine, 84, 95–104,
  106, 133–34, 138–42 *passim*, 150
"Fauna," 152
"Fire," 164
Flowering Dusk (Young), 115
Freedom, 5–6, 55–56, 72,
  83–84
Freud, Sigmund, 5, 80
Frost, Robert, 68
Fury, *see* Wrath

Galileo, 14
Gender issues, 98–104, 105f, 119,
  149. *See also* Sex
Give Your Heart to the Hawks, 28–
  29, 163
God: visions of, by Jeffers, 2, 6ff,
  54–56; in Jesus Christ, 8, 14f,
  74; word of, 9, 12–14, 17, 23,
  105–6, 111–27; conceptualiza-
  tions and, 18; awareness of,
  23–36; wrath of, 47–73, 89–91,
  169; beauty and, 140–48; ap-
  proaching, 168–69. *See also* Ab-
  solute; Christ; *Fascinans*; *Idea of
  the Holy*; *Mysterium tremendum*;
  Nature; Numinous states;
  Religion

"Haunted Country," 43
Hegel, G. W. F., 80
"Hellenistics," 44–45
Hierophanies, 8, 14f, 59, 89
Hippolytus (Euripides), 58
Hotchkiss, Bill, 3
Humility, 75
Hungerfield, 40–42, 71
"Hurt Hawks," 115

Idea of the Holy, The (Otto), 5–8,
  15, 17–22, 43f, 167; salvation in,
  137; the erotic and, 150–65. *See
  also* Absolute; *Fascinans*; God;
  Mysterium tremendum; Numi-
  nous states; Ritual; Sacred
Incest theme, 56, 87f, 122, 153–54
Inhumanism, Jeffers's, 51, 76
Inhumanist, The, 89–92

Jeremiah, 51
Jesus, *see* Christ
John (Apostle), 73
Jung, C. G., 6

Kant, Immanuel, 6

Lawrence, D. H., 151–52
"Local Legend," 39–40
Lommel, Andreas, 113ff
Love, Jeffers on, 35–36
Loving Shepherdess, The, 117–26
  passim

Majestas, tremendum, 11–12, 74–75
"Mal Paso Bridge," 152
"Mara," 19–20, 40, 163
"Margrave," 76–77
Medea, 59–62, 134
"Meditation on Saviors," 35–36,
  135–36
"Meister Eckhart's View of Art"
  (Coomaraswamy), 145–46
Monitor, The (Archdiocese of San
  Francisco), 1–2

Monjian, Mercedes, 2, 4

Moses, 74

Mysterium tremendum, 7, 15, 23–36, 37–39, 57–58, 64, 84f, 98, 125, 138. *See also* Awe; God; Numinous states; Wrath

Mysticism, 5–6, 26–27, 75–89 *passim*, 95–97, 106, 125, 135, 137, 144–46

Mythical themes, 58–59

Myths, Dreams, and Mysteries (Eliade), 7–8

Nature: divinity of, 7, 11–17, 59, 62–64, 138, 142–43, 146, 148–49, 169; and the yearn for the absolute, 129–32

Negativity (negation, nothingness): of Jeffers, 11–12, 17, 46, 51, 81, 85–89 *passim*, 125–27; and *mysterium tremendum*, 25–26; Otto on, 75, 84–86. *See also* Race-naughting; Void

"Night," 44, 99–101, 125

"Nihilism of Mr. Robinson Jeffers" (Wilder), 11–12

"Noon," 165

"Not Our Good Luck," 125

"November Surf," 64

Numinous states, 7–8, 15, 19, 24–25, 38, 44, 98–102 *passim*, 123; God's wrath and, 58–75 *passim*, 84; salvation and, 133–39 *passim*; sex element in, 148, 150f. *See also* Fascinans; God; *Mysterium tremendum*; Mysticism

"Ode on Human Destinies," 142–44

"Oh, Lovely Rock," 103

Only Yesterday (Allen), 49

Other: than self, 18; the wholly, 80–92, 138; beauty's cries for, 141

Otto, Rudolf, *see Idea of the Holy*

Pantheism, 12–17, 146, 169. *See also* Nature

Perret, Frank A., 11–12

"Philosophy and Religion" (Carpenter), 39

Philosophy, Jeffers from perspective of, 2–4, 57

Pliny, 11

Plotinus, 12, 76, 132

Poetry: mysticism and, 95–97; ritual and, 104–5; shaman and, 112–27; religious verse and, *see* Religion

"Point Pinos and Point Lobos," 142–44

Power: awareness of divine, 46, 80. *See also* Awe; *Mysterium tremendum*; Wrath

"Power and Holiness" (Eliade), 7–8

Presbyterianism, Jeffers's, 146

Profane, tension between sacred and, 58–62 *passim*, 82–92 *passim*

Prophet, Jeffers as, 26f, 50, 52, 80, 135, 168–69

Propitiation, ritual, 104–11

Psalms, 62–63

Puritanism, 145f

Race-naughting, 73–80, 124

Radical mentality/consciousness, 74, 167

"Redeemer, A," 32–34, 116

Reduction, in Jeffers, 19–22, 76, 89, 167

Religion: Jeffers, poetry, and, 2–8, 15ff, 26–28, 39–41, 43, 57, 59–73, 82–83, 84, 133, 138, 150, 167–69; experiences of, 5–6, 115–16, 124–25, 139, 142, 145. *See also* Awe; Dread; God; Mysticism; Ritual; Sacred; Sex; Shaman

"Resurrection," 163–64

Retribution motif, 52–53

Rexroth, Kenneth, 136
Ritual: propitiation, 104–11; in idea of the holy, 106–7; shaman's, 112
Roan Stallion, 31–32, 40, 45, 58, 98–99, 115, 126, 154–56

Sacred (the): meaning of, 6–8, 15; tension between profane and, 58–62 *passim*, 82, 85–86, 89–92. *See also* God; *Idea of the Holy*; Religion; Ritual
St. John of the Cross, 26
Salvation, 35–36, 133–37
Sartre, Jean-Paul, 80
Science, Jeffers and, 3–4, 17, 56–58, 89, 92, 135, 168f. *See also* Astronomy
Secularism, 5, 18, 60–61, 68–69
Self-naughting, 77–79
Sex, as element in religious idea, 148–65, 167
Shaman (the), 107, 111–27
Solstice, 54, 60–62, 134–35, 162
Spiritual Aspects of the New Poetry, The (Wilder), 11
Squires, Radcliffe, 3, 49f
Sterling, George, 73
Such Counsels You Gave to Me, 124
Symbols of Transformation (Jung), 6

Tamar, 40, 66, 86–87, 105–6, 109–10, 116–17, 123, 153
"Thebaid," 77–78
Thomas, R. S., 168–69
Thurso's Landing, 71, 162
"To the Rock That Will Be a Cornerstone of the House," 109
"To the Stone Cutters," 52

Tower Beyond Tragedy, The, 40, 52–53, 87, 121–22, 125–26, 139, 153–54
Trance, 112–13, 114, 118, 126
Transcendence, 82, 85–86, 104, 106, 149
Tremendum: majestas, 11–12, 75; element of the, 79. *See also Mysterium tremendum*

Van Doren, Mark, 51–52, 89
Vesuvius Eruption of 1906, The (Perret), 11–12
Violence: Jeffers's holy, 18–19, 49–73, 165, 167, 169; in Scripture, 72–73. *See also* Wrath
Vision, religious, *see* God; Mysticism; Religion
Void (the), 69, 72, 80–81, 83–86, 89, 91–92
"Vulture," 115

Waggoner, Hyatt Howe, 3–4, 135–36
"Whales Weep Not!" (Lawrence), 151–52
Whitman, Walt, 51, 68, 168
Wholeness, 147–48
Wilder, Amos, 11
Winters, Yvor, 71
Women at Point Sur, The, 28, 31, 49–50, 54–56, 64–66, 79, 86, 87–89, 110–11, 122–23, 156–62
Word, God's, 9, 12–14, 17, 23, 105–6, 111–27
Wrath, God's, 47–73, 89–91, 169. *See also* Dread; Violence

Yang/Yin, 98–106 *passim*
Young, Ella, 115